UNIVERSITY OF MICHIGAN
MICHIGAN GOVERNMENTAL STUDIES
NO. 32

COMPETITIVE PRESSURE AND DEMOCRATIC CONSENT

An Interpretation of the 1952 Presidential Election

BY

MORRIS JANOWITZ

*Associate Professor of Sociology
and Research Associate
Institute of Public Administration
University of Michigan*

AND

DWAINE MARVICK

*Assistant Professor of Political Science
University of California (Los Angeles)*

GREENWOOD PRESS, PUBLISHERS
WESTPORT, CONNECTICUT

Library of Congress Cataloging in Publication Data

Janowitz, Morris.
    Competitive pressure and democratic consent.

    Reprint of the ed. published by the Bureau of Govern-
ment, Institute of Public Administration, University of
Michigan, Ann Arbor, which was issued as no. 32 of
Michigan governmental studies.
    Includes bibliographical references.
    1. Presidents--United States--Election--1952.
I. Marwick, Dwaine, joint author. II. Title.
III. Series: Michigan. University. Bureau of Govern-
ment. Michigan governmental studies ; no. 32.
[JK526 1952.J332]   329'.023'730918   75-10214
ISBN 0-8371-8176-3

Copyright © *by The University of Michigan 1956*

Originally published in 1956 by the Bureau of Government,
Institute of Public Administration, University of Michigan

Reprinted with the permission of University of Michigan

Reprinted in 1975 by Greenwood Press,
a division of Williamhouse-Regency Inc.

Library of Congress Catalog Card Number 75-10214

ISBN 0-8371-8176-3

Printed in the United States of America

PREFACE

IN THE current development of social science, the gap between theory and empirical research is particularly marked in the analysis of political institutions. Those who favor systematic research feel that recent advances in methodology are being neglected. Yet political theorists find, in the growing files of empirical data, too few contributions to theory and systematic knowledge.

This analysis of the 1952 presidential election is a conscious, if limited, effort to help close such a gap. It represents an analysis of a body of interview data concerning the 1952 presidential election, collected by the Survey Research Center, University of Michigan. The interpretation of these data is based on a theory of the process of democratic consent.

In analyzing election behavior the survey research approach has usually focused on tracing out the resolution of the vote. Who voted for whom and on what grounds? Our objectives were more in the tradition of viewing elections as a competitive process for maintaining or transferring political authority. We have tried to conduct our analysis on an essentially "political" level. Therefore, the variables relating to social structure and personality had to be translated into the frame of reference of political competition.

The result was that our attention went beyond the examination of political orientations toward parties, candidates, and issues. We were also interested in the processes by which social and psychological predispositions toward the election system were affected by the campaign. What was the impact of interpersonal pressures, of political organizations, of the appeals of mass media? To interpret these data, we had to evaluate these processes in terms of value premises befitting democratic society.

We have tried to be explicit about the criteria by which we judged implications of how the election system operated in 1952. Undoubtedly there will be disagreement about the specific criteria used. But it is our conviction that if empirical techniques are to contribute to the development of political theory, there must be explicit criteria for assessment.

As stated, this analysis is based on data from a national sample survey conducted by the Survey Research Center, University of Michigan. It proceeded under the sponsorship of the Political Behavior Committee of the Social Science Research Council. The authors are grateful to the Center and the Committee for access to their data, but neither the Center nor the Committee bears any responsibility for this analysis.

The organization of the 1952 election survey by the Survey Research Center represents a unique achievement in co-operative group research. The authors wish to express their deep appreciation to Dr. Angus Campbell for so developing the 1952 survey that it met data requirements of a variety of research objectives and yet avoided the dangers of eclecticism. The organization of the study is described in full detail in the preface to the initial report, *The Voter Decides*,[1] by Angus Campbell, Gerald Gurin, and Warren Miller.

Advance planning began well before the election at seminars of Survey Research Center staff members in which the authors were privileged to participate. Besides Dr. Campbell, those present and to whom we wish to express our gratitude were George Belknap, Ben Darsky, James Davies, Elizabeth Douvan, Eugene Jacobson, Warren Miller, Nancy Morse, and Stephen Withey. From the very beginning of these discussions, it became clear that the task of accounting for a candidate's election would yield a significant amount of data by which the quality of the election process could be evaluated.

The political writings of Harold D. Lasswell, as well as his personal comments, were central to our efforts in bridging the gap between political theory and survey research data. Conversations with Samuel Eldersveld on parallel problems continued throughout the entire undertaking. We also received useful comments and assistance from Robert C. Angell, Marshall Knappen, David Reisman, Wilbur Schramm, and Guy E. Swanson.

[1]Evanston, Ill.: Rowe Peterson, 1954.

In addition, we had the benefit of a rewarding critique by a panel of the American Political Science Association at its 1953 meetings in Washington, D.C., where a report on the analysis was presented. Members of that panel included Robert Bower, Heinz Eulau, Harold Gosnell, Ralph Huitt, Fred Irion, Samuel Lubell, and Ralph Straetz.

During the preparation of this monograph, Morris Janowitz served as Research Associate, Institute of Public Administration, University of Michigan. Dwaine Marvick was a postdoctoral fellow of the Carnegie Corporation at the Survey Research Center, and subsequently Lecturer in the Department of Political Science, University of Michigan. Both are deeply indebted to these organizations for the support which enabled them to undertake this analysis. Grateful acknowledgment is also in order for a generous faculty grant-in-aid from the Behavioral Sciences Division of the Ford Foundation.

M. J.
D. M.

CONTENTS

75127

I

THE CRITERIA FOR COMPETITIVE DEMOCRACY

SYSTEMATIC STUDY of the election process has traditionally concerned itself with analyzing the resolution of the vote. What sets of considerations—political, economic, social, and psychological—conditioned the final election outcome?[1] An alternative but neglected task is that of evaluating the election process in terms of the requirements for maintaining a democratic society. To what degree did the election represent a process of consent?

In order to judge how effectively an election expresses the democratic process, a set of rather precise criteria is required. In the eighteenth and nineteenth centuries, theorists assumed self-interest as the basis for rational debate in the democratic electoral process. Out of this assumption grew the so-called mandate theories of democratic elections.

After the Utilitarians, theorists tended to see the key to the process of consent in the conception of "the greatest good for the greatest number." If men were only reasonable, informed, and willing to do their civic duty, the results of self-interested action would inevitably harmonize and further the general welfare. Elected representatives were mere conveniences or nondiscretionary agents. Their instructions from the electorate were clear and mandatory on all major points; their duty was to put those instructions into effect. If an elected representative actually operated as more than a mere agent and was in fact a trustee, his behavior tended to be discounted as a temporary occurrence due to an imperfect election or an unclear popular mandate.

The economic and social circumstances of democratic elec-

---

[1]See Samuel Eldersveld, "Theory and Method in Voting Behavior Research," *Journal of Politics*, Vol. 13 (1951), pp. 70-87, for a summary of election studies.

tions have been undergoing constant change. Profound shifts in these circumstances have forced theorists to offer a markedly different rationale and more explicit prerequisites for political democracy. In a highly complex society, they question the ability of the electorate to formulate clear terms of reference for self-interest, and they observe the growing manipulative potential of mass media and political organizations. In this vein they grow skeptical about the long-term viability of the democratic electoral process. The success of the Nazi Party within the election system of a formal democracy gave actuality to the breakdown of democratic processes through internal pressures.

Contemporary democratic theorists concerned with the inadequacies of the mandate theories have emphasized two neglected aspects of the election process. First, they have underlined its function as a device for choosing officeholders. Victory legitimizes the right to hold office; defeat makes clear the duty to leave office. The election is thus a process of assessing and selecting competing candidates for office. Second, they have emphasized that the election process itself develops attitudes of political compromise and furthers social consensus. For the election is more than the selection of officeholders; it is also part of an institutionalized arrangement for continuous adjustments among competing political and social pressures. As a procedure which is now part of the norms of the political community, the election is an act of civic involvement which can enhance a sense of compromise and thus strengthen political consensus.

Such is the orientation developed by theorists with as diverse assumptions as Pendleton Herring and Joseph A. Schumpeter. In developing standards for judging the American party system, Herring wrote:

> The significance of our system lies not in the alignment of voters pro and con in purely intellectualistic terms but rather in the maintenance of institutions which keep political power contingent and provide alternative sets of rulers. It is well to repeat that in practice our major political parties are primarily concerned not with framing issues and drawing up distinctive programs but in trying to discover

some way of bringing together into a reasonably harmonious relationship as large a proportion of the voters as possible.[2]

In Schumpeter's conception of political democracy, competition between the candidates is made the critical index of democratic elections:

Democracy does not mean and cannot mean that the people actually rule in any obvious sense of the terms "people" and "rule." Democracy means only that the people have the opportunity of accepting or refusing the men who are to rule them. But since they might decide this also in entirely undemocratic ways, we have had to narrow our definition by adding a further criterion identifying the democratic method, vis., free competition among would-be leaders for the vote of the electorate.[3]

Political competition by itself is not enough to secure representative government. Competition only enables the people to choose between alternative leaders who appeal for the privilege of representing them. The electorate, in the same process of disposing of a previous officeholder, votes his successor into power. Thus, if the choice is between demagogues, the electorate suffers; if the choice is between statesmen, the electorate stands to gain. Moreover, as sophisticated critics argue, competitive elections become, more and more, potential devices of mass manipulation. Likewise, it grows harder and harder to produce, by means of elections, the political consensus needed for effective government.

As a result, we must make quite explicit the criteria for assessing the character of political competition. When does the competition of an election produce a "process of consent" which contributes to effective representative government? When does it constitute only a "process of manipulation?" The categories for elaborating such criteria were suggested by the writings of Harold D. Lasswell.[4]

[2]Pendleton Herring, *The Politics of Democracy* (New York: Rinehart, 1940), p.102.
[3]Joseph A. Schumpeter, *Capitalism, Socialism, and Democracy*, (New York: Harper and Brothers, 1943), pp. 384-85.
[4]Harold D. Lasswell, *The Political Writings of Harold Lasswell* (Glencoe, Illinois: The Free Press, 1951). See Bernard Berelson, "Democratic Theory and Public

Initially, three basic conditions have to be assumed about an election before it can be analyzed in detail as to how much consent it represented:

1. A democratic election requires competition between two opposing candidates that pervades the entire constituency. Voters derive power from their ability to choose between at least two competing candidates, either of whom is believed to have a reasonable chance of winning.

2. A democratic election requires both parties to engage in a balance of efforts to maintain traditional voting blocs, to recruit independent voters and to gain converts from the opposition. The need to appeal to these three groups is likely to limit the scope and intensity of campaign competition.

3. A democratic election requires both parties to engage vigorously in an effort to win the current election; but win or lose, both parties still seek to enhance their chances for success in the next and subsequent elections. The process of political competition involves both short- and long-run considerations.

In 1952, the pursuit of victory by both parties was of such an energetic character that one may take it for granted the election corresponded to these assumptions. The relevance of the assumptions is underlined by considerable data from other sources, as well as from this analysis itself. Furthermore, they make it possible to erect more specific criteria for evaluating the political consequences of the competition. To what extent was the competition a "process of mass manipulation" in the 1952 election? Conversely, to what extent was it a process of genuine consent which makes for effective representative government?

It appears that at least five conditions must be met for a competition to make for a process of consent. Each of these criteria has an implied maximum and an implied minimum, to be determined by empirical research. When the criteria are maximized, the potential rationality of voters is enhanced.

Opinion," *Public Opinion Quarterly*, Fall, 1953, pp. 313-30, for an alternative but related set of categories.

When the criteria are minimized, a manipulative election is likely. Hence, these criteria for assessing the quality of a democratic election are directly related to the traditional concern of political scientists with the rationality of the electorate. The five criteria are set forth and elaborated upon below.

1. *The quality of the election depends upon the degree to which competition produces a high level of citizen participation among all social groups.*

Those citizens who vote, regardless of their partisanship, can be said by their efforts to have endorsed the electoral process as an appropriate method for registering popular consent. They have indicated their personal willingness to "play the game," and to accept the outcome according to the rules. The 1952 presidential campaign was not only characterized by intense competition, but also resulted in a high turnout of voters.

2. *The quality of the election depends on the extent to which citizen participation is based on predispositions of high political self-confidence as well as on self-interest in the outcome of elections.*

High turnout alone does not necessarily reflect a process of consent. It may in fact reflect the undesirable effect of mass manipulation or even unstable feelings of desperation. For the "process of consent" there must be appropriate social psychological predispositions underlying the high level of participation.

One social psychological predisposition felt to be crucial is self-interest in the election's outcome. How did the voter feel about the effect of election results on his personal interests? How much did he think voting counted in "the way the country was run?" There is no reason to believe that a theory of the electoral process in a modern mass democracy can differ fundamentally from the classical viewpoint in this respect.

Interwoven with self-interest is self-confidence, as a social psychological predisposition fundamental for the democratic process. How much did the voter feel he could affect public policy through his vote? How well did he feel he understood public issues? Self-confidence implies that the citizen feels that he, and others like him, are able to influence the political process. It implies a basic willingness to abide by the rules of the process and by the consequences of elections. It means, further, that the citizen is realistic about his actual and potential political power, no matter how limited it may be. Self-confidence channelizes self-interest. It stands as a counterweight to the authoritarian way of solving needs of self-interest. Political self-confidence, in turn, reflects deeper personality orientations.

In analyzing democratically oriented participation, it must be pointed out that not all nonvoters are boycotting the electoral process or questioning its fitness as a means to consent. The extent and nature of nonvoting remain to be clarified before political democracy as a symbolic act of consent can be fully understood. There is certainly a level of indifference to the political process which seems compatible with, if not required for, political democracy.

Political analysis also requires the existence of trend data on the level of political participation and predispositions in previous election campaigns. Because the 1952 election study was a first attempt to investigate underlying social psychological predispositions, such trends could not be analyzed, but the base lines are now drawn for comparison with future elections.

Social characteristics and psychological predispositions were analyzed for 1952 in their relationship to particular social and ethnic segments of the electorate. Persons with particular levels of self-confidence and self-interest would be concentrated, it was felt, in particular segments of the socio-economic structure. These predispositions were also expected to be related to shifts in voting behavior from 1948 to 1952. Thus, the central questions were posed: What was the impact of the competition on citizens with low self-confidence and weak self-interest as compared with citizens of converse characteristics? Did the campaign have more influence upon those strongly committed to the democratic process, or upon those at the periphery?

3. *The quality of the election depends on the extent to which competition stimulates effective political deliberation on the issues and candi-*

dates and creates a meaningful basis on which citizens can make their voting decisions.

Mandate theories of democracy emphasize that the electorate must judge all election issues rationally, and on the basis of such deliberation select officeholders who are to have only a minimum of discretion. For a variety of reasons, such a requirement seems unrealistic. In particular, the average person's interest in political questions is probably not sustained enough and he is probably not well enough informed to make such judgments.

Within the framework of competitive democracy, however, the task of the average voter is feasible. He is called upon to weigh the merits of the major issues raised by the contending parties and to reach a "net judgment" as to which side presents the better case for him. He is, moreover, called upon to judge the presidential candidates themselves, as men. For these tasks, the "wisdom of the common man" may well be superior in the long run to any alternative. Lord Lindsay has summed up this view:

> Ordinary plain people have a certain wisdom that is denied to the expert . . . they are the best judges of ends if not means . . . The state will be wisely directed if the final control is in the hands of "ordinary" men—men not specialized in their vocation or training—who have "common sense" and "sound judgment." But those men are, in favorable circumstances, the men to whom others listen, and who furnish the real if informal leadership in a community. The great mass of really ordinary people will follow them, and to give power to everybody by means of universal suffrage is to give power to them. This view . . . implies . . . that the mass of ordinary men and women recognize "sound judgment" and "common sense" in their fellows, and are able to judge a man and ready to approve the natural leader and reject the charlatan.[5]

Thus, the deliberations of the electorate are not limited to campaign issues. Much of the meaningful political deliberation involves weighing the merits of the rival candidates. Since national presidential elections occur only once every four years,

[5] A.D. Lindsay, *The Modern Democratic State* (Oxford, 1943), pp. 276-79.

these estimates of personal stature are in some ways more crucial than are the views of citizens on party programs which are sure to need modification as events change.

Political deliberation which places important emphasis on the merits of rival candidates is quite compatible with competitive democracy reflecting a process of consent. However, to let the quality of the debate be determined solely, or even mainly, by the public image of candidates is to have a fragile basis for political consensus. The quality of the electorate's deliberations was therefore analyzed in terms of the relationship both of issues and candidates to voting patterns.

4. *The quality of the election depends on the extent to which limitations operate precluding either side from monopolizing or even exercising pervasive influence by means of the mass media.*

5. *The quality of the election depends on the extent to which the influence of interpersonal pressures operates substantially independent of the influence of the mass media.*

These last two criteria, dealing with mass media and interpersonal pressures, are so closely interrelated as to warrant joint evaluation. A democratic election implies that both sides are able to make wide use of the means of mass communications and to mobilize extensive interpersonal pressure by means of the party canvass and primary group relations. Nevertheless, the bulk of the electorate must be able to maintain an essential freedom of choice in registering political consent.

For an adequate analysis of the process of consent, some study of the magnitude of the campaign and its penetration is needed. In the past, an absence of reliable information about the scale of penetration has hindered thought on the problems of controlling electoral procedures.

The magnitude of campaign pressures must then be evaluated in terms of the patterns of responses they evoke. But the response of the electorate to the pressures of mass communications and party contact depends on more than institutional and legal controls. The predispositions of the electorate must also operate as safeguards against manipulation. In particular, the climate of opinion in the primary groups—comprising the voter's family and his associates at work—is a crucial mediating influence and has to be investigated.

The foregoing criteria seemed directly relevant for empirical research into the political processes of the modern democratic state.[6] They were formulated to apply to the United States with its present technological and social organization. These criteria are crucial, not comprehensive; they are evaluative criteria, not universally descriptive. But though they are not universally descriptive, it should be possible to use them in analyzing electoral processes in England, France, West Germany, the Low Countries, Scandinavia, and elsewhere. Indeed, they should apply in those national states in which the electoral process satisfies the fundamental requirement for democracy—that of offering the voters a choice between at least two independent and competitive leadership groups seeking office.

In addition, these criteria lend themselves to investigation on the basis of data collected by the sample survey method. The sample survey is a research technique of great usefulness in seeking to understand the dynamics of the electoral process. It is, of course, only one approach. In the past, contributions of the sample survey to an understanding of the electoral process have been mainly descriptive. The 1940 Erie County study by Paul Lazarsfeld, Bernard Berelson, and Helen Gaudet,[7] and the attitudinal analysis of the 1952 national election by Campbell, Gurin, and Miller,[8] are notable exceptions. Utilization of the data as an empirical basis for broad interpretations of the vitality of American democratic institutions is to be found in the study of the 1952 election by Harris, *Is There a*

[6]It does not appear likely that any advantage is to be gained by subsuming these five criteria under a smaller number of headings. The possibility is not precluded, however, that additional criteria may prove necessary to assess the quality of political competition. This can be determined only through additional research and observation.

[7]Paul Lazarsfeld, Bernard Berelson, and Helen Gaudet, *The People's Choice* (New York: Columbia University Press, 1944).

[8]Campbell, Gurin, and Miller, *op. cit.*

Republican Majority?[9] and in Berelson, Lazarsfeld, and McPhee's analysis of Elmira, entitled, *Voting*.[10]

The body of data used in the present analysis represents only a small portion of materials gathered in a larger effort which was undertaken with other objectives in mind. A nation-wide sample was interviewed before and after the 1952 election—first in September and October, and then again in November.[11] The authors believed that survey data could be related to the competitive theory of democracy and thus help to evaluate the strengths and weaknesses of American political practices. The task was to articulate descriptive findings inside a framework that stressed the interplay of campaign pressures and citizen predispositions—social, psychological, and political. The dynamics of the campaign were studied for reasons that extended beyond why voters selected one candidate rather than another. Another equally important question was raised: Was the social consensus, which is indispensable for the democratic process, weakened or strengthened by the election campaign and its results? Since operational measures suggested by the five criteria for a competitive democracy could be constructed, it became possible to estimate how much of a "process of consent" resulted from the campaign of 1952 and to what extent it was a "process of manipulation."

---

[9] Louis Harris, *Is There a Republican Majority?* (Chicago: University of Chicago Press, 1954).

[10] Bernard Berelson, Paul Lazarsfeld, and William McPhee, *Voting* (Chicago: University of Chicago Press, 1954).

[11] See Campbell, Gurin, and Miller, *op. cit.*, for a detailed description of field methodology.

II

THE ARENA OF POLITICAL COMPETITION

THE CHARACTER of political competition for the American presidency and the nature of the resulting political compromise are conditioned by the simple fact that only two parties—and not three or more—are serious contenders for office. From election to election, the arena of political competition varies in terms of the underlying partisanship of the electorate and the extent and intensity of campaign pressures during the struggle.

The 1952 campaign was viewed as a close race in all parts of the nation. In state after state, and locality after locality, a competitive struggle ensued, in varying degree. The pervasiveness of the political competition was as great as, and probably greater than, that in any other American presidential election of modern times.

A crucial index of the intensity of the competition was the feeling of doubt about its outcome, which was widespread throughout the electorate. Nearly half of the electorate felt personally that the outcome in their own state was in doubt, since they expected a close race (see Table I). Another quarter of the electorate simply did not know or would not make a prediction. Only one out of every four persons (26.2 per cent) felt that his own state was assured for one of the two parties. No geographical region was exempt from this uncertainty, since Southerners were as doubtful as Northerners.[1]

Thus the prime requisite for democracy as a working reality—the presence of serious competitors between whom voters may choose—was very much felt to be present in 1952. Not only was the competition intense, but a very large proportion of the electorate thought the race would be close, which put most voters in the position of feeling there was opportunity to influence the election in their own state.

[1]Throughout the text, where a statistically significant difference is reported, it is at least at the .01 confidence limit unless otherwise specified.

TABLE I

"How Close Will the Presidential Election Be
in Your State?"

(Per Cent of Respondents)

Answer	Eastern-ers	Midwest-erners	Western-ers	Southern-ers	Total
A close race......	44.6	48.2	44.7	43.1	45.6
Safe for one party	27.7	31.2	20.2	21.2	26.2
Don't know; won't say	27.7	20.6	35.1	35.7	28.2
Number	(394)	(583)	(199)	(438)	(1,614)

The high level of competition may also account, in part, for the relatively high voting turnout. In all, 61.6 million votes were cast. Depending on the estimated size of the national "residential vote," at least 65.0 per cent and up to 74.2 per cent voted. The findings of the national sample survey on which this analysis is based revealed the close figure of 74.0 per cent who voted (see Table II).[2] Moreover, the distribution of Eisenhower votes to Stevenson votes found in the sample survey (42.5 per cent to 30.6 per cent) again paralleled the actual vote cast.

Expressed as percentages of a national "residential electorate" of 83 million persons, the official voting statistics are comparable to the 1952 voting behavior as found in the national sample survey. Since the national "residential electorate" is

TABLE II

Comparison of Election Statistics and Sample Survey Results
(Per Cent)

	Election Statistics	Sample Survey
Eisenhower voters.........................	40.8	42.5
Stevenson voters	32.9	30.6
Nonvoters................................	25.8	26.0
Other voters	0.5	0.9
Number	(83,000,000)	(1,614)

[2]Based on that portion of the national sample which was interviewed both before and after the election. See Technical Appendix, Section 1, "The Sample of the National Electorate."

an estimate it could have been larger; differences in the sample survey results are probably due to respondents' overreporting the amount of voting.

POLITICAL PARTISANSHIP: BASIC ALIGNMENTS AND SHIFTS

To assess the consequences of political competition during the campaign weeks, some estimate was needed of political inclinations among the American electorate prior to the campaign. It was not enough to compare voting intentions in September and October with voting behavior on election day. Too much of the resolution of political forces had already taken place by early autumn. In some respects, it was more revealing to compare voting behavior in 1952 with that in 1948. Great care had to be taken in such an analysis, however, for no single election lays bare the basic partisan alignment in the country. Each national election is influenced by transitory and episodic factors which detract from its usefulness as a political base line. The starting point needed was some measure of the partisanship with which eligible voters approached the 1952 election; a measure which would reflect long-term and persistent orientations to party symbols.

Partisanship has markedly changed from the 1920's to the 1940's. In the twenties, the United States was basically Republican. A citizen—then, as today—might not always vote Republican; he might split his ticket or he might cast no ballot at all in a particular election. But in his basic inclination, in his personal voting history, in the traditions handed down to him by his parents, if he was politically partisan at all he was probably Republican—that is, in perhaps two cases out of three. To win a national election in the 1920's, it was not enough for Democrats to mobilize the strength of their partisans. An effective appeal to the uncommitted electorate was just as essential for victory. Unless they could make such an effective appeal, the Republican party could, and did, achieve victory. And they did this in an atmosphere of campaign enthusiasm and noise which many students of politics came to think unnecessary, since the electorate was heavily Republican anyway.

By the 1940's, however, most observers agreed that the country had shifted to a basically Democratic partisanship. In election after election the Democrats had been building up and solidifying their core voting strength. Young people were growing up and casting their "first vote" for a Democrat; people were calling themselves Democrats; a steadily growing bloc of voters was emerging, born of parents who thought of themselves as Democrats. Individual citizens may or may not have voted in 1940 or 1944 or 1948. Some of those who voted may have split their tickets or voted as they did because of men or issues peculiar to that election. But if a voter was a partisan, the chances were now about two to one that he was a Democrat.

To measure "partisanship," the sampled electorate was asked whether they considered themselves Republicans or Democrats; for which party they had cast their first vote; and which party their parents favored. On the basis of these questions, the electorate was sorted into Republican "partisans," Democratic "partisans," and the "uncommitted electorate."[3] Because each of these criteria had to be met, a substantial proportion (40.4 per cent) of the electorate fell into the category of uncommitted electors, reflecting the state of American party politics in 1952 (see Table III). At the same time, the data revealed the expected ratio of twice as many Democrats as Republican "partisans": 39.4 per cent to 20.2 per cent.

TABLE III

POLITICAL PARTISANSHIP

	Per Cent	Number
Republican partisans	20.2	325
Uncommitted electors	40.4	655
Democratic partisans	39.4	634
Totals	100.0	1,614.

[3]See Technical Appendix, Section 2, "Operational Definition of Partisanship."

This measure of "partisanship" highlighted the political alignment which produced the Truman victory in 1948, and enabled us to compare it with the realignment that elected Eisenhower (see Table IV). In 1948, Truman won by mobilizing 58.4 per cent of the Democratic "partisans." Of the Democratic "partisans" who did not support him, almost all remained nonvoters, and only a few supported the Republicans (3.9 per cent). Truman also received approximately half of the votes that were cast by the uncommitted electorate. Since nonvoting among the uncommitted electors reached 39.2 per cent, the contest was conditioned fundamentally by the relative proportions of Democratic and Republican "partisans." The Republican campaign failed either to mobilize the necessary votes from the uncommitted electorate or to convert Democratic "partisans."

In 1952, however, instead of merely dividing the uncommitted electorate, the Republicans got 43.2 per cent of its votes compared with Stevenson's 24.0 per cent (see Table IV). Even more important was the fact that the Republican competition resulted in having almost two out of every seven Democratic

TABLE IV

POLITICAL PARTISANSHIP AND THE PRESIDENTIAL VOTE, 1948-1952
(Per Cent)

	Republican Partisans	Uncommitted Electors	Democratic Partisans	Total
1948 Election				
Dewey voters	75.7	24.4	3.9	26.7
Truman voters	4.9	32.7	58.4	37.1
Nonvoters.	17.8	39.2	33.6	32.7
Other and not ascertained	1.6	3.7	4.1	3.5
1952 Election				
Eisenhower voters .	83.1	43.2	21.1	42.5
Stevenson voters . .	2.5	24.0	51.9	30.6
Nonvoters	13.8	31.3	26.7	26.0
Other and not ascertained	0.6	1.5	0.3	0.9
Number	(325)	(655)	(634)	(1,614)

partisans who voted in 1952 cast their ballots for Eisenhower.

The end results of Republican campaign efforts and the corresponding failure of Democratic strategy are more clearly revealed by tracing voting patterns throughout the two elections (see Table V). Of the potential voting population, 46.5 per cent were regular party voters (Republican, 1948 and 1952 = R – R; Democratic, 1948 and 1952 = D – D). Each party had about half of these on its side. Persistent nonvoters amounted to 16.1 per cent (Nonvoter, 1948 and 1952 = NV – NV). All told, 29.6 per cent of the electorate were classified as changers—those who from 1948 to 1952 either switched parties, were mobilized, or dropped out (R – D, D – R, NV – R, NV – D, R – NV, D – NV).[4]

These changers were the citizens whose voting behavior produced the new voting alignment of 1952. Only 8.4 per cent of the electorate *changed* in such a way as to improve Stevenson's position, while 21.2 per cent, by their *change*, contributed to Eisenhower's victory. Specifically, those who shifted from the Democratic to the Republican candidate outnumbered the Republicans who switched to the Democratic candidate by about ten to one (D—R's, 10.2 per cent of the electorate; R—D's, 1.0 per cent). The number of 1948 nonvoters who were mobilized for Eisenhower (NV—R), however, was only half as great as the number of Truman voters who switched to Eisenhower (NV—R's, 5.0 per cent; D—R's, 10.2 per cent).

A political party grows and prospers not merely when its "partisans" continue to register votes in its favor but also when uncommitted electors and even "partisans" of the opposition shift their support to it. How much of the pro-Eisenhower vote came from its own "partisan" ranks if the pro-Eisenhower vote was defined as the R — R's, D — R's, and NV — R's *plus* the D — NV's ? To Republicans it is a vital sign that 63.1 per cent of those whose voting behavior was pro-Eisenhower consisted of persons who were not already Republican "partisans" (as

---

[4]The very small per cent (3.9) who were minors in 1948 are included in this definition, since the parties were faced with the special task of mobilizing them into the electorate and committing them politically for the first time.

TABLE V

Political Partisanship and Presidential Voting Patterns, 1948-1952

| Presidential Voting Patterns | | Political Partisanship | | | Total | | Per Cent Total Electorate |
1948 Vote	1952 Vote	Republican Partisans (Per Cent)	Uncommitted Electors (Per Cent)	Democratic Partisans (Per Cent)	(Per Cent)	Number	
Pro-Republican behavior							
R	R	59.2	35.6	5.2	100.0	(386)	23.9
D	R	5.5	46.6	47.9	100.0	(165)	10.2
NV	R	24.7	50.6	24.7	100.0	(81)	5.0
D	NV	3.3	27.4	69.3	100.0	(62)	3.8
Pro-Democratic behavior							
D	D	1.3	31.2	67.5	100.0	(365)	22.6
R	D	11.7	58.9	29.4	100.0	(17)	1.0
NV	D	1.5	35.4	63.1	100.0	(65)	4.0
R	NV	51.8	48.2	0.0	100.0	(27)	1.7
1948 minors							
Minor	R	25.8	51.3	22.9	100.0	(35)	2.2
Minor	D	0.0	10.8	89.2	100.0	(28)	1.7
Minor	NV	9.1	41.8	49.1	100.0	(55)	3.6
Nonvoters							
NV	NV	8.5	56.1	35.4	100.0	(260)	16.1
Unclassifiable		10.2	48.6	41.2	100.0	(68)	4.2
	Totals....					1,614	100.0

defined above). By contrast, Democrats must face the fact that 63.2 per cent of those whose voting behavior was pro-Stevenson were Democratic partisans. The Democrats were, so to speak, thrown back upon their reserve strength. And finally, Democrats should find it discouraging that among partisans who failed to vote in both elections, there were four Democrats to every Republican.

These details may suggest to some the beginning of an increase in the bloc committed to Republican partisanship. However, in 1956, the Republicans must again wage an intensive competitive battle among the uncommitted and even among Democratic partisans. The Republican victory in 1952 presages that the task may be less difficult, but it does not erase the primary fact that, among partisan citizens, it is still the Democratic party two to one.

GEOGRAPHICAL STRONGHOLDS

A different perspective on the magnitude of the Republican victory, and on the nature of the coalition behind it, shows up in the political complexion of localities from which our nationwide sample was drawn. Nearly one-fifth of the representative sample lived in Republican strongholds, two-fifths in localities where the parties were fairly evenly matched, and two-fifths in Democratic strongholds. Half of the Democratic strongholds were in the South.[5] These proportions of party strongholds are roughly the same as the proportions of political partisans in the electorate at large.

The competitive aspects of the campaign were undoubtedly enhanced by the fact that uncommitted electors appeared in about the same proportions in the four types of communities. In Southern strongholds of the Democratic party, as in the other types of communities, roughly one-third of the electorate was uncommitted.

The Republican strongholds produced the greatest plurality

---

[5]See Technical Appendix, Section 3, "Operational Definition of Geographical Strongholds."

TABLE VI

GEOGRAPHICAL STRONGHOLDS AND THE
1952 PRESIDENTIAL VOTE
(Per Cent)

	Republican Strongholds	Competitive Areas	Democratic Strongholds		Total
			Northern	Southern	
Eisenhower voters	59.7	45.6	42.3	23.3	42.9
Stevenson voters	26.0	31.6	40.1	25.2	30.9
Nonvoters	14.3	22.8	17.6	51.5	26.2
Number	(300)	(647)	(319)	(334)	(1,600*)

*Does not include fourteen persons "not ascertained."

for Eisenhower in 1952, the competitive areas next, and the Democratic strongholds, North and South respectively, the least (see Table VI). But whereas the Stevenson vote rose from Republican strongholds to Northern Democratic strongholds, it fell off precipitously in Southern Democratic strongholds. Yet this was not because of a corresponding rise in the Eisenhower vote in the South, but rather because of the markedly larger proportion of nonvoters found there.

CAMPAIGN PRESSURES IN THE POLITICAL ARENA

The next step in our description of the arena of competition was to examine the pattern of penetration by major campaign pressures. From the second series of interviews completed shortly after election day, a body of data was gathered which made it possible to analyze the consequences of interlocking and overlapping patterns among these pressures.

Six measures of campaign pressure were investigated as follows: (1) mass media patterns of exposure to campaign news; (2) mass media involvement; (3) political party canvassing; (4) personal campaign activities; (5) political preferences of friends and co-workers; and (6) political preferences of immediate family.

The sheer magnitude of these pressures served to highlight both the extensive penetration of the campaign and the intensity of competition. Initial examination of these data showed clearly that Republicans held a superior position over Democrats; they were more successful in exposing their partisans to campaign pressure from the mass media, and even in mobilizing informal political activities on their own behalf. Republicans likewise operated with a relative advantage in exposing their partisans to interpersonal influence, and had even greater access to the uncommitted electorate in this respect (see Table VII and Table VIII).

The network of the mass media constituted the most extensive instrument of campaign activities. Patterns of exposure reflected the rapid but still incomplete diffusion of television that had occurred by the summer of 1952. In measuring involvement with the mass media of television, radio, or newspapers, we distinguished between fans, ordinary viewers, listeners or readers, and nonusers.[6] Only 6.4 per cent of the entire electorate were wholly unconcerned with the mass media, while the comparable percentage for uncommitted voters was 10.8 per cent (see Table VII). On a projection from the sample electorate, only 5.3 million citizens were wholly unconcerned with the election content of the mass media.

In the new world of television, the Republicans had an initial advantage: coverage and content on behalf of Eisenhower outweighed that of Stevenson. Both the traditional bent of those who controlled the mass media and the greater efforts of the Republican party were responsible.

In addition, the sample survey disclosed that Republican partisans were more likely to be exposed to the channels of mass communications than Democratic partisans. Among Republican partisans, 72.7 per cent were preoccupied enough with the political content of the mass media to be classified as fans, whereas the proportion for Democratic partisans was only 57.0 per cent. The uncommitted electorate had a pattern of

[6]See Technical Appendix, Section 4, "Operational Definitions of Mass Media Exposure and Involvement," for the details of this measure.

TABLE VII

Political Partisanship and Mass Media Involvement*
(Per Cent)

	Republican Partisans	Uncommitted Electorate	Democratic Partisans	Total
Television fans......	28.0	22.9	24.8	24.8
Radio fans	24.0	18.8	18.8	19.8
Newspaper fans	20.7	12.7	13.4	14.6
Total fans	72.7	54.4	57.0	59.2
Television users.....	6.8	7.5	9.9	8.4
Radio users.........	7.7	12.8	11.4	11.3
Newspaper users.....	8.3	10.5	10.7	10.4
Total users	22.8	30.8	32.0	30.1
Other media	11.1	6.0	5.5	8.4
Nonusers; not ascertained	2.8	10.8	8.7	6.4
Number	(325)	(655)	(634)	(1,614)

*Totals add up to more than 100 per cent because of a few fans or users of more than one medium. This holds true for all subsequent tables involving mass media involvement.

TABLE VIII

Political Partisanship and Campaign Pressures
(Per Cent)

	Republican Partisans	Uncommitted Electors	Democratic Partisans	Total
Proportions of the electorate:				
Canvassed	13.5	11.7	12.1	12.3
Not canvassed	86.5	88.3	87.9	87.7
Active in campaign..	40.7	26.2	30.9	31.2
Not active.........	59.3	73.8	69.1	68.8
Friends and co-workers are:				
Pro-Eisenhower ...	58.5	54.0	19.5	32.0
Pro-Stevenson	5.2	18.6	31.5	20.6
Mixed—Neutral ..	36.3	27.4	49.0	47.4
Immediate family is:				
Pro-Eisenhower ...	71.0	36.9	19.0	38.4
Pro-Stevenson	4.6	19.1	42.0	26.8
Mixed—Neutral ..	24.4	44.0	39.0	34.8
Number	(325)	(655)	(634)	(1,614)

involvement somewhat less intensive than the Democrats (54.4 per cent).

These data also document the greater involvement of both Republican and Democratic partisans with television as compared with either radio or newspapers as their source of political orientation. In fact, the 1952 campaign witnessed a dramatic use of television as a crucial forum, with the result that its audience exceeded that of newspapers and radio.

Supplementing coverage through the mass media was the contacting and canvassing by the major political parties. The data on canvassing (see Table VIII) referred only to personal visits and telephone calls by party workers, although doubtless both parties also relied upon handbills, postcards, and so forth.

Considering only such canvassing, it was found that 12.3 per cent of the nationwide sample was visited by one or both parties, 3.3. per cent by both. Because of the sampling methods employed, this meant that 12.3 per cent of the households sampled were canvassed.

The Republican canvass was at least as large as the Democratic one, if not larger. Fully 53.0 per cent of all major-party canvassing reported was attributed to Republican party-workers. One might have expected the Democratic party to have outstripped its rival in the use of canvassing as a campaign technique. This might have been inferred both from the two-to-one Democratic partisanship of the electorate and from the known importance of canvassing as a campaign technique employed by metropolitan Democratic organizations. Yet the Republicans seem to have reached as many if not more potential voters than did the Democrats.

Republicans also had a competitive advantage over the Democrats in being able to mobilize a larger proportion of their basic partisans into informal campaign activities such as giving money, attending rallies, actively "talking politics" or working for a candidate. In all, these types of campaign activities involved 31.2 per cent of the electorate, far exceeding the number of people reached by the political canvass. Of the Republican "partisans," 40.7 per cent were so involved, whereas, of the Democratic "partisans," 30.9 were active.

Of course, in absolute terms, the advantage was still with the Democrats. Roughly eight million Republican partisans were active personally during the campaign, compared with over eleven million Democrats.

Finally, the data concerning primary group pressures on the voter revealed that Republicans led Democrats in mobilizing extensive word-of-mouth support for their candidate. For the nation as a whole, more electors reported they were subject to interpersonal influence from friends, co-workers, or family in support of Eisenhower than in support of Stevenson.[7] It was no surprise, of course, that among partisan Republicans, concertedly pro-Stevenson interpersonal pressure from friends and co-workers was almost wholly absent (5.2 per cent). But the converse, which was also expected, was not the case. Almost one out of every five Democratic partisans was subject to concerted Republican pressure from friends and co-workers. Among the uncommitted, pressure from these sources was in a majority of cases (54.0 per cent) pro-Eisenhower, and only in a minority (18.6 per cent) pro-Stevenson. Pressures from family members operated with a similar imbalance.

The resulting advantage which Republicans derived from interpersonal pressure probably exceeded that from any other type of campaign pressure. Undoubtedly, the personal appeal of Eisenhower was a primary factor in mobilizing such widespread, informal, word-of-mouth support. The extent to which even Democratic partisans were shown to be subjected to this type of interpersonal pressure is indeed impressive. At various points throughout this study, the findings throw some light on the dynamics of this personal appeal.

In summary, in order to evaluate the consequences of the election, the first criterion investigated was: The quality of the election depends upon the degree to which competition produces high levels of citizen participation. The percentage of

[7]See Technical Appendix, Section 10, "Operational Definition of Interpersonal Pressure."

the electorate which cast its ballot produced a relatively high level of participation reversing what some observers have seen as a steady downward trend in American voting turnout. It was more crucial, however, that the electorate in fact believed that the decision was in doubt and that it therefore was selecting a president from two contenders, each one of whom had a real possibility to win.

The campaign operated on an electorate in which, as traditionally, the uncommitted partisans predominated, and in which the Democrats had come to outnumber the Republicans (there were approximately 40 per cent uncommitted, 40 per cent Democratic, and 20 per cent Republican). The resulting Republican victory was based to a larger extent on the conversion of 1948 Truman voters than on the mobilization of the 1948 nonvoters.

The intensity in the political competition no doubt contributed to the level of turnout. The mass media, and, in particular, the newly developed television system, transmitted this intense competition to the electorate. Only a minute minority—6.4 per cent—could be described as genuinely unconcerned with the public discussion generated by the campaign. The grass-roots activity of house canvassing, intense though it may have been, only touched a minority of the electorate, perhaps a quarter at best. Strangely enough, in terms of sheer coverage, the Republicans reached at least as many potential voters as the Democrats by this technique. In addition, the Republicans had the advantage in mobilizing primary group word-of-mouth pressures.

But in this campaign, or in campaigns in general, the fact that the Republicans succeeded and the Democrats failed in achieving the necessary levels of participation means relatively little as far as democratic consent is concerned. Was the participation distributed throughout the various social groupings or was it dangerously concentrated in some? Moreover, the second criterion must be considered in the analysis, the criterion which is concerned not with the amount of participation but with the underlying predispositions conditioning the participation.

III

THE 1952 ELECTORATE: SOCIAL CHARACTERISTICS AND PSYCHOLOGICAL PREDISPOSITIONS

A PERSON'S STATUS, whether based on his social class or his ethnic-religious grouping, has long been held to condition his political behavior fundamentally. We may assume that the demands people tend to make, and the ways they expect "politics" to affect their lives, are strongly influenced by the social groups they belong to and identify themselves with; their view of "politics" is equally affected by how much confidence they have in their own ability to take part in political affairs. Thus it was important to chart as precisely as possible the social class and ethnic-religious composition of the 1952 presidential vote for comparison with that of the 1948 vote.

Likewise, psychological predispositions of the electorate regarding politics seemed crucial for relating political behavior to the stability of a competitive democracy. Two social psychological measures for which data were collected were political self-confidence and calculations of political self-interest.[1] It was assumed that these predispositions would have different consequences for voting behavior in different social classes and different ethnic-religious groups. Their investigation would enable us to evaluate the second criterion for competitive democracy: An election must involve high levels of participation based upon predispositions of political self-confidence as well as self-interest in the outcome of elections.

SOCIAL STRATIFICATION OF THE ELECTORATE

Our measure of the social class of households in the national sample was constructed with both occupation and income as

[1] See Technical Appendix, Section 5, "Operational Definition of Self-Interest in Elections," and Section 6, "Operational Definition of Political Self-Confidence." It will be noted that this measure conceptualized and operationalized differently from the measure of "sense of political efficacy" in *The Voter Decides*.

25

TABLE IX

SOCIAL CLASS AND THE 1952 PRESIDENTIAL VOTE
(Per Cent)

	Upper-Middle	Lower-Middle	Upper-Lower	Lower-Lower	Farmers	Total*
Eisenhower voters	65.0	51.8	32.7	24.9	43.3	42.5
Stevenson voters..	23.9	28.7	43.3	29.7	24.4	30.6
Nonvoters	10.3	18.6	23.3	44.7	31.1	26.0
Other; not ascertained	0.8	0.9	0.7	0.7	1.2	.9
Number	(263)	(327)	(420)	(273)	(196)	
Total						(1,614)

*Total includes 135 cases for which voting behavior could not be classified into social class.

criteria. It was also possible to divide the sample according to ethnic-religious affiliations.[2]

First, it emerged that the Eisenhower vote in 1952 was directly and progressively related to social class: the higher the social class, the greater the concentration percentagewise of the Republican vote (see Table IX). The range was from 65.0 per cent of the upper-middle class through 51.8 per cent of the lower-middle and 32.7 per cent of the upper-lower to 24.9 per cent of the lower-lower class. The farmers fell appropriately between classes, with 43.3 per cent of them Republican voters. By contrast, the Democratic concentration rose as social class fell, with the critical exception of the lower-lower class, where the highest concentration of nonvoting for any social class reversed the trend line. The Stevenson vote rose from 23.9 per cent of the upper-middle class and 28.7 per cent of the lower-middle to 43.3 per cent of the upper-lower class. However, it fell to 29.7 per cent in the lower-lower class.

Second, it was clear that ethnic-religious groupings contributed to the Eisenhower victory in markedly different degrees (see Table X). American politics has long been characterized by the prominence of such voting blocs, and the 1952 presi-

[2]See Technical Appendix, Section 7, "Operational Definition of Social Class and Ethnic-Religious Groupings."

TABLE X

ETHNIC-RELIGIOUS GROUPINGS AND THE 1952 PRESIDENTIAL VOTE

	Negroes	Jews	Catholics	Nominal Protestants	Church-going Protestants	Total*
Eisenhower voters	6.4	25.0	41.2	47.5	56.8	42.5
Stevenson voters..	26.1	65.5	43.5	26.5	23.4	30.6
Nonvoters	66.9	7.7	14.4	25.4	19.8	26.0
Other; not ascertained	0.6	1.8	0.9	0.6	0.0	.9
Number	(157)	(52)	(338)	(677)	(337)	
Total						(1,614)

*Total includes fifty-three cases for which voting behavior could not be classified in ethnic-religious groupings. Negroes were excluded from the religious classification.

dential election was no exception. How the Negro or Jewish vote would go, how the Catholics would align themselves politically, how church-going Protestants would differ from nominal Protestants: these have traditionally been key questions for the practical politician.

When the Protestant population was divided into church-going and nominal adherents, it was found that 56.8 per cent of all church-going Protestants and 47.5 per cent of all nominal Protestants in the American electorate were Eisenhower supporters. On the other hand, Stevenson was supported by only 23.4 and 26.5 per cent, respectively.

Among the so-called "minority groups"—Catholics, Jews, and Negroes—Stevenson received a plurality of the votes cast. However, in the case of the largest of these groups, the Catholics, the traditional advantage given to a Democratic candidate was almost lost. Eisenhower was able to garner 41.2 per cent of the Catholic electorate, thus falling only a little short of Stevenson, who got 43.5 per cent of its potential support.

Stevenson's pluralities among Jews and Negroes were much more impressive. Fully 65.5 per cent of the Jews voted for Stevenson, whereas only 25.0 per cent backed Eisenhower.

75127

Among the Negroes, 26.1 per cent voted for the Democratic candidate, compared with 6.4 per cent who favored Eisenhower. But nonvoting among the Negro electorate was markedly greater than for any other group. In the nation as a whole, 67.3 per cent of the Negroes did not vote; in Southern Democratic strongholds, 90.0 per cent of them took no part in the election. Consequently, although the Negro population vastly exceeds the Jewish population and both minorities gave huge pluralities to Stevenson, the Democratic candidate probably received almost as many votes from Jews as from Negroes. It may also be noted that the amount of voting in the lower-lower class and among Negroes failed to reach the appropriate minimum levels for competitive democratic politics.

SOCIAL CLASS AND VOTING REALIGNMENTS

By comparison with a preceding election, the strength of a political party in a current election is made up of its regular party voters plus those whose voting behavior changed in the party's favor. This "party plurality" in a particular social class is the sum of its "regular party advantage" and its "net party gain." In the voting realignments from 1948 to 1952, the Republicans registered gains and the Democrats suffered losses in all social classes. However, Eisenhower's victory was clearly brought about by his pluralities in the middle class.

In 1952 the Republican party's strength from regular voters (R − R's) was heavily concentrated in the middle class, and the Democratic party's regular strength (D − D's) tended to come from the lower class (see Table XI). Moreover, the magnitude of the gains for Eisenhower was progressively related to social class. To show this, we measured the magnitude of the "net party gain" for Republicans in 1952 over 1948 (see Table XII). In each class, the action of some changers was cancelled out by the action of others. The "net" Republican gain was that remaining proportion of a class which effectively increased Eisenhower's plurality, after subtracting the off-setting action of pro-Stevenson changers.

TABLE XI

SOCIAL CLASS AND VOTING REALIGNMENTS
(Per Cent)

	Upper-Middle	Lower-Middle	Upper-Lower	Lower-Lower	Farmers	Total*
Regular Republican voters....	45.2	30.9	16.6	15.0	24.4	24.9
Regular Democratic voters ...	18.7	21.9	32.6	24.0	19.6	23.6
Pro-Eisenhower changers	22.7	25.5	21.7	14.6	24.0	22.3
Pro-Stevenson changers	7.1	8.1	12.1	7.5	7.6	8.9
Persistent nonvoters	6.3	13.6	17.0	38.9	24.4	20.3
Number	(252)	(310)	(405)	(254)	(184)	(1,546)
Not ascertained ..						(68)
Total						(1,614)

*Total column includes 135 cases for which no adequate social class data could be ascertained.

In the upper-middle class, this effective contribution to Eisenhower's victory was made by 15.6 per cent; in the lower-middle class, it was slightly higher—17.4 per cent. However, in the upper-lower class the net Republican gain was only 9.6 per cent, and in the lower-lower class it was only 7.1 per cent. In terms of numbers as well as of proportions, the voting changes in the lower-middle class made the largest contribution to Eisenhower's victory. The 1952 election was thus a victory for

TABLE XII

SOCIAL CLASS AND THE BASIS OF PARTY PLURALITY
(Per Cent)

	Upper-Middle	Lower-Middle	Upper-Lower	Lower-Lower	Farmers
Regular party advantage ...	26.5 (R)	9.0 (R)	16.0 (D)	9.0 (D)	4.8 (R)
Net party gain..	15.6 (R)	17.4 (R)	9.6 (R)	7.1 (R)	16.4 (R)
Party plurality..	42.1 (R)	26.4 (R)	6.4 (D)	1.9 (D)	21.2 (R)

the middle class; this may be seen from the fact that Eisenhower received plurality support only in the upper-middle and lower-middle classes and among the farmers, although Stevenson's margin of superiority in both lower-class groups was small.

Clearly, the coalition of the upper-lower class with the lower-middle class—the basis of Democratic success for two decades—was upset in 1952 (see Table XIII). It was replaced by a coalition of the lower-middle class with the upper-middle class.

TABLE XIII

SOCIAL CLASS AND THE PARTY MAJORITY
(Per Cent)

	Upper-Middle	Lower-Middle	Upper-Lower	Lower-Lower	Farmers
Ratio of Majority to Minority Party Vote:					
1948 Democratic coalition	42.9	55.5	73.0	65.9	58.0
1952 Republican coalition	73.4	64.4	42.9	46.0	63.9

This new coalition apparently achieved power because of the high incidence of nonvoting in the lower-lower class (where Stevenson received only a bare plurality) and because of the shift in the farm vote, where the Republicans registered a net gain of 16.4 per cent.

POLITICAL SELF-CONFIDENCE AND SELF-INTEREST

Although class and ethnic-religious affiliations were clearly related to voting decisions in 1952, it was also assumed that some measure of social psychological predispositions would have to be applied to the American electorate. Citizens with similar positions in the social structure often differ in evaluating the democratic election process and vote differently in consequence. Measures of underlying predispositions toward politics were, therefore, required—in particular, measures of political self-confidence and of self-interest in the outcome of the election.

In introducing such measures it was not intended to explain away findings about the class and ethnic-religious group bases in American politics. It is unfortunate that these new variables—generally of a social psychological nature—are sometimes used to supplant rather than to elaborate traditional analysis of political behavior. This results not only in a neglect of important empirical findings but also in oversimplified theories of political change. Our purpose in using such variables was rather to qualify basic findings about the voting behavior of social strata. The underlying assumption was that comparable patterns of self-interest and self-confidence in politics will have different consequences for different social classes and for different ethnic-religious groupings.

How did political self-interest and self-confidence condition the formation of the Republican coalition in 1952? A battery of four questions permitted rough division of the sampled electorate into those who acknowledged strong self-interest in the outcome of elections, and those who expressed only weak self-interest. Another battery of four questions divided them roughly into those with high and low political self-confidence, respectively.

The question arose as to whether, in measuring self-interest, political self-confidence was not also reflected. If it had been, one dimension could have substituted for the other, or have been subsumed by the other. But empirically, the two dimensions were found to be highly independent of each other. Thus, a four-way grouping of the electorate was developed, based on the two critical dimensions. Those with high confidence and strong self-interest were characterized as "effective citizens" while those with high confidence and weak self-interest were viewed as "indifferent citizens." Those manifesting low confidence and strong self-interest were considered to be "involved spectators" and, finally, those with low confidence and weak self-interest were referred to as "apathetic persons."

	Political Self-Confidence	Election Self-Interest
Effective Citizen	High	Strong
Indifferent Citizen	High	Weak
Involved Spectator	Low	Strong
Apathetic Person	Low	Weak

This typology provided an instrument for gauging the relative impact of mass media and campaign pressures on one social grouping rather than another. Citizens with low political self-confidence and weak self-interest were expected to be more vulnerable to mass manipulation.

Like social class and ethnic-religious affiliations, these types appear to have set the limits within which the competitive aspects of the campaign had effect. Social psychological pre-dispositions were found to have a direct relation to patterns of voting behavior. Pro-Republican changers—persons who voted Republican in 1952 but not in 1948—proved with statistical significance to be less likely than regular Republican voters to be effective citizens (see Table XIV). On the other hand, among

TABLE XIV

A. Voting Realignments and Types of Political Citizens (Per Cent)

	Regular Republican Voters	Pro-Republican Chg'rs	Regular Democratic Voters	Pro-Democratic Chg'rs	Persistent Non-voters*	Total
Effective citizens	34.1	24.2	34.8	31.2	15.9	28.5
Indifferent citizens	35.9	31.5	28.8	29.6	16.6	27.6
Involved spectators	13.9	17.4	16.3	18.4	26.9	18.9
Apathetic persons	16.1	26.9	20.1	20.8	40.6	26.0
Number	(386)	(343)	(365)	(137)	(315)	(1,546)†

B. Breakdown of Pro-Republican Changers (Per Cent)

	D−R's	NV−R's‡	D−NV's
Effective citizens....................	26.1	20.8	27.4
Indifferent citizens	34.5	31.3	16.1
Involved spectators	12.1	15.7	32.3
Apathetic persons...................	27.3	32.2	24.2
Number	(165)	(116)	(62)

*Includes fifty-five nonvoters who were minors in 1948.

†Total excludes sixty-eight cases for which no basis for classification of 1948-52 voting pattern could be ascertained.

‡Includes thirty-five Eisenhower voters who were minors in 1948.

pro-Democratic changers the concentration of effective citizens was quite close to that found among regular Democratic voters.

At the opposite extreme, among apathetic persons, the reverse picture emerged for Republicans. Pro-Republican changers were with statistical significance more likely than regular Republican voters to be apathetic persons, whereas among pro-Democratic changers and regular Democratic voters no differences were revealed in the concentration of apathetic persons. Specifically, it was found that, among Truman voters who switched to Eisenhower (D – R's), among nonvoters in 1948 who were mobilized to Eisenhower (NV – R's), and among Truman voters who dropped out in 1952 (D – NV's), the incidence of apathetic persons was disproportionately high.[2]

Thus, a key characterization of the new sources of Republican strength can be made. The dynamics of competitive democracy in 1952 appear to have penetrated to the periphery of the American electorate. Each of those elements of the electorate who shifted their support to the Republican party (D – R's, NV – R's, and D – NV's) included disproportionately small concentrations of effective citizens and disproportionately large concentrations of apathetic persons. The new Republican

---

[2]There is good reason to believe that political self-confidence reflects deeper personality tendencies. A small subsample of the respondents was administered a battery of ten questions designed to measure authoritarian personality tendencies. Some questions were derived directly from the F scale employed by the Berkeley group and others were adapted from those employed by F. Sanford. Unfortunately the number of cases was too small to use extensively in the present analysis. It is interesting, however, that the predicted positive relationship between high political self-confidence and low authoritarian tendencies actually held true to a statistically marked degree. See Adorno, T. W., *et. al.*, *The Authoritarian Personality* (New York: Harper and Brothers, 1950), and Sanford, Filmore, *Authoritarianism and Leadership* (Philadelphia Institute for Research in Human Relations, 1950).

	High Political Self-Confidence Per Cent	Low Political Self-Confidence Per Cent
High authoritarian	21	42
Intermediate	42	37
Low authoritarian	37	21
Number	(272)	(184)

majority came about through a disproportionate recruitment of those voters with low political self-confidence and weak self-interest in the election outcome. Each of these factors suggests a proneness to yield to manipulative pressures and an inability to use independent judgment in politics.

THE DYNAMICS OF PARTY PLURALITIES: SOCIAL CLASS AND PSYCHOLOGICAL PREDISPOSITIONS

The assumption was made earlier that social class would condition the consequences of political predispositions on voting behavior. An analysis was therefore required of the dynamic composition of party pluralities, with a simultaneous consideration of social class and political predispositions (see Table XV).

It will be recalled that a "party plurality" is the sum of that party's "regular party advantage" and its "net party gain." Analysis indicated that Republicans had a stable party advantage, in terms of regular voters—much greater among high confidence persons of the upper-middle, lower-middle, and farmer classes than among low confidence persons of corresponding status. Conversely, the Democrats had a stable advantage much greater among high confidence persons in the upper-lower class than among their low confidence counterparts. In the lower-lower class, with its high degree of nonvoting, no clear-cut difference emerged. An even more striking cleavage along class lines emerged when the analysis was made in terms of self-interest in the election outcome.

Among the stable participants in the electoral process, therefore, social class and political predispositions combined to establish party advantages running clearly along class lines. However, when we analyzed "net party gains" by examining voting shifts from 1948 to 1952, a striking difference was revealed in the conditioning effects of political predispositions, class by class. In the upper-middle class the net party gains for Eisenhower were considerably more pronounced among low confidence citizens (29.8 per cent) than among high confidence citizens (10.6 per cent). The same was true, although less

TABLE XV

(Per Cent)

	Upper-Middle	Lower-Middle	Upper-Lower	Lower-Lower	Farmers
Stable Party Advantages *					
High self-confidence .	30.3 (R)	12.5 (R)	22.1 (D)	7.8 (D)	24.7 (R)
Low self-confidence .	15.6 (R)	2.0 (R)	7.2 (D)	9.7 (D)	1.0 (D)
Strong self-interest ...	38.1 (R)	12.5 (R)	23.6 (D)	14.5 (D)	2.6 (D)
Weak self-interest ...	17.6 (R)	5.7 (R)	9.7 (D)	3.8 (D)	10.5 (R)
Net Party Gains †					
High self-confidence .	110.6(R)	14.0 (R)	9.2 (R)	14.7 (R)	12.3 (R)
Low self-confidence .	29.8 (R)	24.4 (R)	10.3 (R)	3.0 (R)	19.3 (R)
Strong self-interest ...	9.1 (R)	14.3 (R)	8.6 (R)	4.9 (R)	13.9 (R)
Weak self-interest ...	20.4 (R)	20.3 (R)	10.6 (R)	9.2 (R)	18.1 (R)
Total Party Pluralities ‡					
High self-confidence .	40.9 (R)	26.5 (R)	12.9 (D)	6.9 (R)	24.7 (R)
Low self-confidence .	45.4 (R)	26.4 (R)	5.1 (R)	6.7 (D)	18.3 (R)
Strong self-interest ...	47.2 (R)	26.8 (R)	15.0 (D)	9.6 (D)	11.3 (R)
Weak self-interest ...	38.0 (R)	26.0 (R)	0.9 (R)	5.4 (R)	28.6 (R)

*Stable party advantages are calculated by subtracting the proportion of a class which consists of regular Democratic voters (D-D's) from the proportion which consists of regular Republican voters (R-R's) or vice versa.

†Net party gains are calculated by subtracting the proportion of a class which consists of pro-Stevenson changers (R-D's, NV-D's, and R-NV's) from the proportion which consists of pro-Eisenhower changers (D-R's, NV-R's, and D-NV's).

‡Total party pluralities are calculated by adding the net party gains in a given class to the stable party advantages found to prevail in that same class.

pronouncedly, in the lower-middle class (24.4 per cent of the low confidence citizens here were registered as net Republican gains, compared with 14.0 per cent of the high confidence citizens in this group). In the upper-lower class, the net Republican gains came almost equally from high and low confidence citizens (10.3 per cent of the low confidence types and 9.2 per cent of the high confidence persons). Only in the lower-lower class, with its relatively minor contribution to the Republican victory, did the net Republican gains among high confidence citizens (14.7 per cent) exceed proportionately the gains among low confidence citizens (3.0 per cent). In essence, this confirms the earlier findings that crucial components of the Eisenhower voting realignment (the three subtypes classified as pro-Eisenhower changers) were characterized by low levels of self-confidence and tended to come from upper social groups. It is also clear from Table XV that the net Republican gains were due in large part to pro-Republican changers characterized by weak self-interest in the election outcome.

Thus the Republicans not only depended upon continuing to attract high confidence and strong interest voters from upper social groupings; their victory also called for a successful appeal to low-confidence and weak-interest voters coming disproportionately from the same social strata. These low-confidence and weak-interest elements of the middle class seem particularly important to future political realignments in American elections and therefore require extended analysis by political scientists. It seems reasonable to assume that they include those elements of society which have repeatedly been pointed to as being highly sensitive to social dislocation and prone to extremist politics.

These observations are confirmed when we examine the joint effects on voting behavior of self-confidence and self-interest, class by class. A pattern also emerges which helps in understanding voting realignments in terms of the interplay between social group factors and psychological predispositions. If the two political parties are viewed as having basic and manifest relationships to the class structure and ethnic-religious grouping of the electorate, then two sets of responses conditioning voting behavior seem to operate. On the one hand, individuals who *regularly* adopt the voting pattern typical of their social class or ethnic-religious grouping may be expected to be relatively confident and self-interested in politics, so far as personal predispositions are concerned. On the other hand, individuals who only sporadically conform to the voting pattern typical of their social group may be expected to be relatively lacking in self-confidence and self-interest in elections.

TABLE XVI

VOTING REALIGNMENT, SOCIAL CLASS, AND TYPE OF POLITICAL CITIZENS
(Per Cent)

	Regular Republican Voters	Pro-Eisenhower Ch'ngers	Regular Democratic Voters	Pro-Stevenson Ch'ngers	Persistent Non-voters	Total*
Middle Class						
Effective citizens	42.8	22.1	34.8	32.5	24.1	33.4
Indifferent citizens	36.7	37.5	38.2	41.8	31.1	37.1
Involved spectators ...	11.9	14.7	12.2	9.3	20.7	13.3
Apathetic persons	8.6	25.7	14.8	16.4	24.1	16.2
Number	(210)	(136)	(115)	(43)	(58)	(562)
Lower Class						
Effective citizens	21.0	28.8	35.8	32.4	15.4	26.6
Indifferent citizens	31.4	27.2	23.8	19.1	16.1	23.2
Involved spectators ...	19.0	18.4	18.2	22.1	26.2	20.8
Apathetic persons	28.6	25.6	22.2	26.4	42.3	29.4
Number	(105)	(125)	(193)	(68)	(168)	(659)

*Analysis excludes 393 cases for which no basis for classification was available.

In Table XVI it appears clearly that the "effective citizens" of the middle-class—those with high political self-confidence and strong self-interest in elections—were far more apt to be regular Republican voters (42.8 per cent) than to be pro-Eisenhower changers (22.1 per cent). But this was true only in the middle class. Among "effective citizens" of the lower class, the tendency was in the opposite direction, although with too few cases the findings did not reach statistical significance.

At the other extreme, the incidence of "apathetic persons" in the middle class—those with low political self-confidence and weak self-interest in elections—was higher to a statistically significant degree among pro-Eisenhower changers (25.7 per cent) than among regular Republican voters (8.6 per cent). Again, among "apathetic persons" of the lower class, the opposite tendency appeared.

Thus, in the middle class, those who regularly voted in accordance with their class interest—assuming the Republican party to be middle-class oriented—were citizens with relatively strong psychological predispositions concerning politics. On the other hand, those who were sporadic conformers to the politics of their class—persons who occasionally failed to con form in the past and who returned to Republicanism in 1952—were citizens with relatively weak psychological predispositions concerning politics. It was these latter elements of the middle class whose voting changes made possible the Republican victory.

In the lower class, voting patterns do not emerge clearly as responses of social psychological predispositions. A number of considerations may help to explain this class difference. It is likely that the functional and symbolic importance of politics to the middle-class citizen is generally higher than for lower-class citizens. It was therefore probable that a victorious Republican candidate had to appeal not only to the regular champions of, and sporadic conformers to, Republicanism in the middle class, but also to those lower-class citizens whose aspirations make them receptive to middle-class symbols of authority and leadership, whatever their basic social psychological predispositions.

To summarize, the analysis of the social characteristics of the electorate helped further to evaluate the first criterion of a competitive election, namely, the need for high level of voting participation. When analyzed by social groupings, the adequate over-all level of voting participation revealed a marked failure to vote in the lower-lower social class and among the

Negro population.   These same data highlight the social stratification basis of the Republican victory.   The higher the social
class, the greater was its concentration of the Republican vote,
and, moreover, the higher the social class, the greater proportionately was its shift in 1952 to Eisenhower.

By the use of a battery of questions on political self-confidence
and election self-interest, the extent to which the second criterion was not met emerged.   To what extent was citizen participation based on predispositions of high political self-confidence as well as self-interest in the outcome of the elections?
There can be no doubt that the political competition penetrated
to the periphery of the self-confident and self-interested voters.
The pro-Eisenhower changers were characterized by a disproportionately high concentration of low self-confidence and weak
self-interest voters.   Only by collecting trend data from one
election to another will it be possible to evaluate the significance
of the over-all level of political self-confidence and election self-
interest that we encountered in the electorate.   However, it is
clear that the consequences of these underlying predispositions
vary from social class to social class.   It was in the middle class
that the bulk of the pro-Eisenhower changers was constituted of
voters with low political self-confidence and weak election self-
interest.

IV

THE QUALITY OF THE ELECTORATE'S
DELIBERATION

THE ELECTION of a president as a result of a two-party campaign means in effect that the electorate has only one real decision to make. Nevertheless, meaningful deliberation in any presidential campaign requires voters to weigh two types of considerations. This was especially true in the 1952 campaign.

On a rational level, deliberation centered around the issues and the political rhetoric of the campaign. The quality of such deliberation could be judged by the extent to which voters become involved in debating and weighing those issues. What patterns of attitudes toward campaign issues could be found in the various strata of the voting population? A sample survey, with its emphasis on the scientific neutral investigation of discrete issues, rules out any extensive analysis of the dynamics of political deliberation. Perhaps with a more argumentative approach to respondents, more appropriate data could have been gathered. But such an emphasis would have meant the sacrifice of other basic objectives. Actually, only a few of the central issues could be investigated, namely those on which the parties were known to divide. Moreover, the survey was necessarily confined to collecting a concise expression of attitude on each issue.

On an emotional level, the campaign deliberation focused heavily on the public personality and imagery of the opposing candidates. Voters were called upon to make a deliberate choice between the candidates as political leaders, as standard bearers of their party, and as human beings. Although deliberations about candidates can involve overtones of irrationality and emotionalism, such deliberations are still relevant to a theory of competitive democracy. Again, the sample survey method of research has only limited opportunities for probing deeply into the respondent's images and subjective evaluations of candidates as symbols of authority.   But a content analysis of the interview enabled us to distinguish generalized attitudes toward Eisenhower and Stevenson and to relate such attitudes to voting preferences.

The quality of citizen deliberation on issues had also to be judged indirectly.   A pattern of attitudes on key campaign issues which was consistent with the announced position of one party could be viewed as a meaningful basis for a voting decision. A pattern of attitudes which either revealed no basis for preferring one party's position over another's, or which indicated preference for one party's position as often as the other's, could be construed as providing no meaningful basis for a voting decision.   To what degree, then, were attitudes on party-framed issues of public policy related to voting alignments in 1952? Indirectly, it was the answer to this question which enabled us to assess the quality of deliberation during the campaign.

Since the relative importance of political issues as compared with candidate appeal has long preoccupied practical politicians, it likewise promised to supply a basis for analysis of campaign deliberation.   Throughout the campaign, strategists of both parties apparently were concerned with a proper emphasis and balance.   Communications via the mass media during the campaign, the appeals pressed by the local party organizations, and the arguments that took place in intimate face-to-face groups fell, in good measure, on one side or the other of this central dichotomy: the merits of the men and the merits of the issues.

Likewise, a theory of competitive democracy requires some *a priori* judgment about what is a proper concern by the electorate over political issues versus the character of the candidates.   If the election is a process of arriving at consent which must endure post-election realities, how is the final agreement aided or hindered by the electorate's over-emphasis or underemphasis of either issues or candidates?   The problem takes on particular meaning within the American constitutional system, where the relationship between the President and Congress is not mediated by explicit and formal parliamentary institutions.

In the 1952 election, since General Eisenhower was without previous political commitment, such considerations were of added importance.

According to the premises of traditional democratic theory, it is issues that are crucial. After rational analysis based on self-interest, the electorate selects officeholders who within reasonable limits are committed in their political program. It is precisely this aspect of the process of consent which the critics of democracy consider most susceptible to "mass manipulation." Broad segments of the population, they argue, are unable to formulate their self-interest in clear political terms. Often, too, when these segments are able to formulate self-interest, it lacks even a rudimentary political consistency and so cannot be related to alternatives posed by the two major parties.

The criteria of competitive democratic elections also require a minimum consistency between issues and political choice in an election. However, this relationship is now seen as secondary. Instead, greater emphasis is placed on the competition between candidates and on the imagery of candidates as sponsored by the rival parties. The election is primarily a means by which officeholders are selected. Only in a secondary sense is it appropriate as a means of expressing self-interest on public issues. Therefore, less consistency between issue orientation and voting behavior was to be expected. In theory, moreover, more inconsistency can be tolerated as compatible with competitive democracy.

In the simplest terms, a two-step analysis (of voting behavior, attitudes toward issues and attitudes toward candidates) was expected to throw light on the quality of campaign deliberation and the quality of consensus it developed. First: What patterns of attitudes toward key issues were found among Eisenhower voters as opposed to Stevenson voters? No causal analysis was directly envisioned; yet it was necessary to chart how extensively each set of voters held attitudes that were clear cut and consistent with their party's position. Second: Was there evidence, as might be expected, of a closer link between candidate imagery and voting choice than between party-framed ideology and voting choice?

CAMPAIGN ISSUES AND THE 1952 VOTE

Specific controversies did, of course, present powerful appeals to particular segments of the population. Individual campaign issues were almost certain to divide a considerable number of Republicans from Democrats. Some of these issues were peculiar to the campaign of 1952; others were of long standing.

For example, the corruption issue, embodied in part in the slogan, "Time for a Change," was heavily underscored throughout the campaign. Our data, however, indicate that it was an issue that aroused the concern of only a minority of the electorate. No specific or direct question dealing with corruption was contained in the interview schedule. Concern over this issue was measured by a content analysis of spontaneous mentions, since the interview was repeatedly so structured as to bring comment on that topic. In all, 389 respondents (24.2 per cent of the total sample) made spontaneous mention of corruption and, by implication, indicated it was a factor to be weighed in their choice. Only 51 (13.1 per cent) took a position on the corruption issue that could be characterized as pro-Democratic; by contrast, 338 (86.9 per cent), more than six times as many, expressed a pro-Republican attitude.

Of those who took a pro-Republican viewpoint on the corruption controversy, over three-quarters (76.9 per cent) voted Republican, while of those who took a pro-Democratic stand, only half (50.9 per cent) voted for Stevenson. The implications of the corruption controversy as a conditioner of Republican voting behavior will be amplified later, when a fuller analysis is made of the other key campaign issues (see Table XX).

By contrast with the corruption issue, spontaneous expressions of concern with internal communism were considerably fewer. Only 59 respondents (3.7 per cent of the sample) mentioned it spontaneously, less than one-sixth as many as spoke of corruption in government. The political implication was almost completely one-sided; all but four respondents took a pro-Republican stand. Crude though these measures may be, they are a useful guide to the relative weight of the two controversies in the deliberations of the electorate.

While these two issues were specific for the 1952 campaign, a core of long-standing issues was presented to the voters reflecting years of strategic competition between the two parties. During the last two decades, the Democratic party had sponsored a wide range of social welfare policies. How did the vote for Stevenson and for Eisenhower relate to the major elements of the New Deal heritage? One would expect at least a preponderantly favorable orientation toward these issues on the part of Stevenson voters. Foreign policy was more complex, since the Republicans had developed a stake in bipartisanship and since Eisenhower had not in effect repudiated the goals of bipartisan foreign policy. Nevertheless, even in the area of foreign policy, a difference in attitudes was to be expected between Eisenhower and Stevenson voters.

Seven questions—three on domestic policy and four on foreign affairs—were used in the pre-election schedule to gauge attitudes on party-framed issues. The three domestic issues dealt with: (1) social welfare activities of the national government; (2) legislative action to ensure fair employment practices; and (3) legislative revision of the Taft-Hartley labor law. The four issues of foreign policy were concerned with: (1) the extent of United States involvement in world affairs, (2) the degree of American responsibility for the loss of China to the Communists, (3) the correctness of the United States entry into the Korean war, and (4) the best current policy to pursue in Korea.[1]

Tables XVII and XVIII classify the Eisenhower and Stevenson vote according to the voter's attitude on the specific issues. These data highlight the proportion of the electorate whose opinions had crystallized in favor of one party's stand, and simul-

[1]See Technical Appendix, Section 8, "Ideological Orientation Toward Campaign Issues," for the full text of questions.

TABLE XVII

THE 1952 PRESIDENTIAL VOTE AND DOMESTIC CAMPAIGN ISSUES
(Per Cent)

	Eisenhower Voters	Stevenson Voters	Non-voters
Governmental Social Welfare Activity			
Should do more (alternative formulations)	19.5	34.0	22.6
About right; O.K. as is	37.8	54.6	51.5
Should do less (alternative formulations)	31.7	5.4	10.3
More on some, less on others	3.9	.7	1.2
Don't know; not ascertained	7.1	5.3	14.4
Revision of Taft-Hartley Law			
Completely repealed	6.7	28.1	8.6
Changed in favor of labor (alternative formulations)	2.6	5.1	1.4
Changed in favor of management, with minor pro-labor changes	36.0	12.5	10.7
Other changes	6.5	5.5	2.6
No knowledge of Taft-Hartley Law	48.2	48.8	77.7
F. E. P. C.			
National government should legislate	18.5	30.5	25.0
State government should legislate	15.9	14.8	13.6
Government should take an interest, not ascertained how	4.9	5.1	10.0
Government non-legislative action only	7.6	8.5	7.4
National government should stay out but state government should take action	19.8	13.4	10.3
National and state government should stay out entirely	20.7	16.6	16.9
Favor restrictive action	5.7	4.5	5.3
Don't know; not ascertained	6.9	6.6	11.5
Number	(687)	(494)	(419)

taneously measure the divergence on these issues between Eisenhower and Stevenson voters. Since opinions were gathered largely in October, prior to actual voting, the attitudes reported may be taken to represent in good part the relevance of these issues to voting decisions.

It is perhaps a mark of America's acceptance of its role in

TABLE XVIII

THE 1952 PRESIDENTIAL VOTE AND FOREIGN POLICY CAMPAIGN ISSUES
(Per Cent)

	Eisenhower Voters	Stevenson Voters	Non-voters
U.S. Foreign Involvement			
Country has not gone too far......	28.2	43.3	26.5
Pro-con	1.6	3.0	2.6
Country has gone too far..........	65.6	45.8	50.6
Don't know; not ascertained.......	4.6	7.9	20.3
U.S. Entry into Korean War			
Yes, we did the right thing........	34.6	52.8	33.7
Pro-con	6.7	3.8	5.0
No, we should have stayed out.....	46.2	32.7	42.7
Don't know; not ascertained.......	12.5	10.7	18.6
1952 U.S. Korean Policy			
Keep trying for a peaceful settlement	36.8	52.4	51.8
Pull out of Korea entirely.........	9.5	6.5	11.7
Take a stronger stand and bomb Manchuria and China	46.4	35.2	27.2
Don't know; not ascertained	7.3	5.9	9.3
U.S. China Policy			
Nothing we could do	38.4	61.5	48.7
It was our fault.................	38.5	18.2	11.0
Don't know; not ascertained	23.1	20.3	40.3
Number	(687)	(494)	(419)

world politics that rudimentary ideological patterns on questions of foreign policy were at least as firmly crystallized as on matters of domestic policy. Moreover, despite the efforts of Eisenhower and his leading followers to narrow the range of competition on foreign issues, the ideology of his supporters diverged from that of Stevenson in foreign policy to a degree equal to, if not greater than, that encountered in domestic politics.

On the question of social welfare activity by the national government, only a very small percentage had no opinion (8.4 per cent of the total sample and 6.3 per cent of those who voted; see Table XVII). The extent of consensus on the developments of the New Deal was reflected by the finding that more than half of the Eisenhower supporters were willing to accept Democratic social welfare policies. Likewise, almost 90 per cent of the Stevenson supporters were willing to accept the social welfare policies of the Administration as sufficient to meet their needs. On the other hand, 31.7 per cent of the Eisenhower voters demanded a retrenchment of social welfare activity while only 5.4 per cent of the Democrats had that attitude.

The ideological outlook with respect to labor problems presented a markedly different pattern. Slightly less than a majority of the voters had no crystallized opinions on modification of the Taft-Hartley Act (48.2 per cent of the Eisenhower voters and 48.8 per cent of the Stevenson voters). Of the Eisenhower voters, 6.7 per cent were in favor of complete repeal, while among Stevenson supporters the percentage was 28.1.

Specific responses to the F.E.P.C. issue need to be evaluated with great care, since the same response had markedly different political overtones in different regions of the country. The range of responses was rather highly differentiated in general, with only moderate differences between Republican supporters and Democratic supporters as compared with their responses on other domestic issues of social policy. This reflects the complex character of opinion on the F.E.P.C. issue.

Attitudes toward the level of U.S. foreign involvement divided Eisenhower voters from Stevenson voters almost as much as any single domestic issue (see Table XVIII). Of the Eisenhower voters, 65.6 per cent expressed agreement with the anti-Administration proposition that "this country has gone too far in concerning itself with problems in other parts of the world." Only 45.8 per cent of the Stevenson voters were of this opinion. Attitudes were crystallized in party-framed terms to the extent that a relatively low concentration of Eisenhower voters and Stevenson voters alike fell into the "no opinion" category (4.6 per cent and 7.9 per cent, respectively).

Korea emerged as a most crucial aspect of the campaign deliberation. Despite Eisenhower's pronouncements, the initial intervention of the United States in Korea remained a controversial subject.   His supporters included 46.2 per cent who believed that the United States should not have intervened. Current (1952) policy in Korea divided the electorate in a similar pattern.   The data suggest that Eisenhower represented a compromise position on Korea acceptable to citizens whose views were markedly different.   A majority of his supporters (55.9 per cent) voiced opposition to the Truman Administration's policy of continuing to work for an armistice.   They consisted of two highly divergent blocs.   One bloc wished the United States to pull out of Korea entirely (9.5 per cent) while the larger group (46.4 per cent) wanted to take a stronger stand, bombing Manchuria and China.   Eisenhower's promise of a personal inspection of the Korean battlefield apparently appealed to both groups of voters dissatisfied with the stalemated situation.   In particular, he was appealing to persons who had low levels of personal tolerance for the ambiguous struggle and who desired clear-cut action.

Finally, on. the issue of .U.S. responsibility for the loss of China, on which more people had "no opinion" than any other foreign issue investigated, there was a similar differentiation between Eisenhower and Stevenson supporters.   Of the Stevenson vote, 61.5 per cent took a pro-Administration view on this matter, while only 38.4 per cent of the Eisenhower vote absolved the Truman Administration.

THE IDEOLOGICAL BASIS OF POLITICAL COMPROMISE

By combining attitudes on specific domestic and foreign issues, we were able to evaluate the quality of campaign deliberation in terms of broader political ideology.   Ideology was conceived of as a pattern of attitudes toward a range of fundamental issues, using expressed party platforms as the basic criteria.   In constructing this measure of ideology, only five of the seven issues were used.[2]   For the purposes of this analysis,

[2]In the foreign affairs sphere, the question of U.S. intervention in Korea was eliminated as being repetitious of the issue of the 1952 policy in Korea.   F.E.P.C. was eliminated from the domestic issues, since the responses were widely scattered and linked to overriding regional interpretations that made evaluation on a national basis overly complex.

responses to these issues were coded as pro-Democratic Administration, neutral or no opinion, and anti-Democratic Administration. Although there were disadvantages to such an analysis,
it did measure ideological deviation from the 1952 Administration policy.

Four categories of ideological orientation were employed:

"*Stalwarts*"—those who supported the party position on all or almost
    all of the issues
"*Compromisers*"—those who supported the party position in a majority
    of the issues
"*Weak Compromisers*"—those whose support was limited to a minority
    of the issues, with a tendency to have no opinions or contradictory
    opinions on the remainder
"*Ambivalent or Neutralized*"—those who were divided on the majority
    of the issues, neutral on almost all of the issues, and in some cases
    with no opinion[3]

Thus, in Table XIX, the presidential vote is classified by the
electorate's compromise position on these two domestic and
three foreign issues.

TABLE XIX

THE 1952 PRESIDENTIAL VOTE AND IDEOLOGICAL ORIENTATION
(Per Cent)

	Eisenhower Voters	Stevenson Voters	Non-voters	Total*
Republican stalwarts	16.7	1.1	3.0	8.3
Republican compromisers..	26.2	8.4	8.4	16.0
Weak Republican compromisers	17.2	11.0	18.8	16.0
Ambivalent or neutralized ..	16.5	20.2	22.0	19.0
Weak Democratic compromisers	11.1	20.4	27.5	18.0
Democratic compromisers ..	10.4	21.7	16.6	15.4
Democratic stalwarts	1.9	17.2	3.7	7.3
Number	(687)	(494)	(419)	(1,600)

*Total excludes fourteen cases for which no basis for classification was available.

[3]See Technical Appendix, Section 8, "Ideological Orientation toward Campaign
Issues," for details of the classification scheme and the operational definitions of the
category system.

We recognize that these issues represented only a sample of the range of policy alternatives on which the parties were divided. We also recognized that arbitrary definitions were used to establish meaningful categories of political orientation. But given these limitations, it was still felt that the categories contributed to a more meaningful analysis of a competitive theory of democracy.

From the outset, it was clear that to find a large segment of the electorate in the "stalwart" category was neither to be expected nor even desired if the election was to be a process of consensus and compromise. In general, it is necessary to underline the contributions to the competitive arena of "compromisers" and even "weak compromisers." In this type of analysis, simple negative value judgments toward voters who show a relative lack of opinion on crucial issues gives way to a clearer understanding of how compromise may develop. "No opinion" is therefore not regarded as an inherent evil, per se; danger only arises when exceptionally high levels of "no opinion" or contradictory opinion prevent meaningful consensus. In any case, one must avoid the simplistic fallacy of assuming that the holding of fixed party-framed opinions on all subjects is the desirable criterion for evaluating political deliberation in a campaign.

It was found that only 16.7 per cent of the Eisenhower voters were Republican "stalwarts" in that they supported the Republican party position on all or almost all of the issues. The percentage of Stevenson voters who were Democratic party "stalwarts" was about the same, 17.2 per cent. Any assumption that the Republican voters had a decidedly higher ideological consistency than the Democratic voters is dispelled by this and subsequent observations from the data. Since the party stalwarts represented heavy and therefore rigid commitment to the "party line," a greater concentration of voters in these categories could have hindered the process of consent through elections. Nevertheless the major political parties must draw much of their stable support and organizational strength, as well as intellectual vitality, from the ranks of these party stalwarts.

A party's stalwarts must be augmented by the less doctrinaire "compromisers"—those who at polling time show an explicit position of compromise on which they base their candidate preference. In a society as dynamic and diverse as that of the United States, these compromisers represent important components of the electorate. Thus, of Eisenhower's voters, 26.2 per cent were Republican "compromisers," while Stevenson's voters included 21.7 per cent Democratic "compromisers." It seems reasonable to assume that the bulk of the Republican compromisers would vote persistently for the Republican candidate, and the same would be expected of Democratic compromisers. Nevertheless, the image of the candidate, campaign pressure, and other considerations led small but important minorities to vote for the candidate opposed to their ideological inclination.

However, those voters classified as "weak compromisers" reflect an ideological orientation that seems too undefined for effective political competition. They were the individuals who, by and large, saw little fundamental difference between the alternatives posed by the two principal parties competing for the right to rule. In all, 29.5 per cent of those who cast a vote for president were of this type in 1952. Yet the fact remains that weak Republican compromisers voted two-to-one for the Republican candidate, while weak Democratic compromisers voted for Stevenson only to a slightly greater extent than for Eisenhower. Thus, while the voting behavior of these groups was not random, both parties seem likely to have extended their claims by over-simplification and extremism in order to appeal to such groups, which, in this sense, constitute a potential pressure for at once over-intensifying and weakening the competitive process.

The range of ideological orientations is completed by the neutrals, who constituted 16.5 per cent of the Eisenhower voters and 20.2 per cent of the Stevenson voters. For the members of this group, campaign competition seems to have failed to create a link between party-framed alternatives and their personal ideological demands.

The pattern of linkage between voting behavior and ideological orientation can be summarized in another way by comparing persistent party voters with party changers. These data confirm previous findings, based on the analysis of political predispositions, that the political competition reached the periphery of the electorate. Those voters who were pro-Republican changers (between 1948 and 1952) appeared markedly less explicit in their ideology than persistent Republican voters. Thus, for example, the combined incidence of Republican stalwarts and Republican compromisers among regular Republican voters was 53.3 per cent; the combined incidence among the pro-Republican changers was only 24.8 per cent. The extent to which the shift to Eisenhower was based on considerations other than issues is further delimited by the fact tht 18.9 per cent of the pro-Republican changers were Democratic compromisers and 3.6 per cent of them were even Democratic stalwarts. A similar but somewhat narrower gap was present between pro-Democratic changers and regular Democratic voters in their ideological orientations.

Finally, these patterns of ideological orientation afforded an over-all device for making inferences about how significantly certain campaign issues affected voting behavior.[4]   In particular, there was the question of how much impact lay in the corruption controversy. As mentioned earlier, almost a quarter of the sampled electorate expressed concern about the corruption issue, and this concern rested on attitudes which were exploitable by Republicans. Those who expressed concern were characterized by an overwhelmingly pro-Republican orientation (86.9 per cent to 13.1 per cent).

In order to gauge how far the "corruption issue" was able

---

[4] A breakdown of the over-all ideological patterns into the groups of domestic and foreign issues revealed similar results in both cases to those of the combined analysis.   One noteworthy difference, however, was the higher concentration of ambivalents and those without orientation in foreign policy matters, as compared with that of weak compromisers.   The concentration was almost equal for both parties.

TABLE XX

IDEOLOGICAL ORIENTATION, CORRUPTION, AND
THE 1952 PRESIDENTIAL VOTE
(Per Cent)

	Republican Stalwarts	Republican Compromisers*	Neutrals	Democratic Compromisers*	Democratic Stalwarts	Total†
No concern about the corruption issue: Eisenhower voters.......	76.2	48.4	29.9	23.3	11.3	34.1
Stevenson voters	8.9	24.0	34.4	39.3	72.2	34.7
Nonvoters	14.9	27.6	35.7	37.4	16.5	31.2
Number	(67)	(362)	(247)	(442)	(97)	(1,215)
Pro-Republican concern about the corruption issue: Eisenhower voters.......	85.1	86.5	72.9	57.0	26.6	77.1
Stevenson voters	1.6	6.4	18.7	23.6	66.7	13.7
Nonvoters	3.3	7.1	8.4	19.4	6.7	9.2
Number	(61)	(141)	(48)	(72)	(15)	(337)

*Includes both compromisers and weak compromisers.
†Excludes sixty-two cases for which no basis for classification was available.

to offset ideological orientation which was otherwise pro-Democratic, persons with similar ideological leanings who expressed no concern with this issue were contrasted with those who did (see Table XX). The results lead to the inference that in 1952 corruption was an important Republican appeal which served to motivate a small group of persons who might otherwise have been expected to vote for Stevenson. In all ideological groups, a pro-Republican concern with the corruption issue mobilized a higher Eisenhower vote, even at that end of the ideological continuum most heavily committed to the Democrats. The greatest impact was among the ideologically neutral, as might have been expected.

COMPETITION AND CANDIDATE IMAGERY

As opposed to the complex relations between ideology and presidential vote, the linkage between candidate imagery and presidential vote was almost "one-to-one." The endless pre-occupation of the mass media with the human interest aspects of the candidates undoubtedly contributed to the formation of these images.

Charting the electorate's imagery of the two candidates is a tedious and complex matter. The more direct the approach, the less likelihood that the interview will produce candid and revealing insight into the underlying and emotionally charged imagery and stereotypes about Eisenhower and Stevenson. Therefore, the data on imagery were not gathered as responses to direct or "structured" questions, but from the two interview sessions which lasted about one hour each and covered a wide range of political topics; this gave ample opportunity for those interviewed to reveal spontaneously and indirectly their images of the two candidates. The verbatim records of the interviews were carefully analyzed for content, and responses were classified in a range from strongly pro-Eisenhower to strongly pro-Stevenson (see Table XXI). The classification scheme depended on the balance of positive to negative (favorable to unfavorable) references accorded to one candidate or another.[5] Thus, this operationalization is different from that presented in the Survey Research Center's basic report, *The Voter Decides.*

The expected correspondence between imagery and presidential vote was not only extremely high, but there were no significant exceptions or revealing deviations. To be sure, the incidence of those who held a strongly favorable image of their candidate was somewhat higher among Eisenhower voters than among Stevenson voters (39.0 per cent to 32.7 per cent). But if those voters who had mildly favorable imagery of their candidates are included in order to arrive at over-all

[5] See Technical Appendix, Section 9, "Operational Procedures for Analysis of Candidate Imagery."

TABLE XXI

THE 1952 PRESIDENTIAL VOTE AND CANDIDATE IMAGE
(Per Cent)

	Eisenhower Voters	Stevenson Voters	Non-voters	Total*
Strongly pro-Eisenhower ...	39.0	5.2	21.0	24.0
Mildly pro-Eisenhower.....	21.2	3.2	4.6	11.3
Ambivalent or neutralized..	22.8	17.8	15.4	19.3
Mildly pro-Stevenson	4.0	30.9	12.1	14.4
Strongly pro-Stevenson	2.0	32.7	21.0	16.4
None†	11.0	10.2	25.9	14.6
Number	(687)	(494)	(419)	(1,600)

*Total excludes fourteen cases for which no basis for classification was available.
†Since the categorization of imagery depended on the balance expressed between the two candidates, the "None" category included 6.7 per cent who revealed an image of only one candidate.

totals of favorable imagery, both candidates were quite equal. However, additional light on the impact of Eisenhower's public personality is shown by the fact that about twice as many voters who held ambivalent images of both candidates voted for Eisenhower as for Stevenson. In the past, the United States has had civilian presidential leadership during all of its armed conflicts. Military heroes as presidential candidates have assumed power in periods after the military conflict or crisis. In 1952, while military operations were being carried on, the persistence of international tension apparently resolved the old ambivalence toward military candidates in Eisenhower's favor.

Moreover, the concentration of ambivalent or neutral imagery among Eisenhower supporters was not only greater than among Democratic supporters, but also exceeded the concentration among nonvoters. Here was a form of cross pressure which, apparently because of its character, did *not* lead to nonvoting. And finally, nonvoters included the highest concentration of those who held no imagery. Apparently, favorable imagery toward Stevenson was more compatible with nonvoting than favorable imagery toward Eisenhower, an additional criterion affirming the impact of Eisenhower's public personality.

The third criterion for evaluating the election hinged on the consequences of the political deliberation stimulated by the campaign. The measure was not "political man," fully and consistently committed to one party on all campaign issues. Rather, did the political deliberation create a meaningful basis on which citizens could make their voting decisions? Both issues and candidates had to be considered.

The analysis, in summary, demonstrated that the presidential vote was closely and consistently linked to images of the presidential candidates. Nevertheless, almost one-fifth of the electorate revealed a candidate imagery that was neutral or ambivalent, suggesting that they made their voting decision from other bases.

Furthermore, the political deliberation over central campaign issues must be evaluated as failing to develop a basis for some particular groups on which to ground their decision. A range of campaign issues—domestic and foreign—make possible a classification of the voters into "stalwarts," "compromisers," "weak compromisers," and "ambivalent neutrals" with respect to Republican and Democratic party programs. Each group had a contribution to make to the functioning of the electoral process and thereby to the form of consensus that emerged. Even the weak compromisers had some notion about the style of government they preferred. However, for the ambivalent neutrals— 16.5 per cent of the Eisenhower vote and 20.2 per cent of the Stevenson vote—the campaign failed to link party-framed alternatives, personal ideological demands, and voting behavior. Though it cannot be said that this group acted without any deliberation as to its self-interest, its members were most vulnerable to the manipulative aspects of the campaign. The dynamics and limitations of the deliberative process can be stated alternatively: the pro-Republican changers between 1948 and 1952—those who effected a change in political power—showed markedly lower levels of ideological orientation than did the persistent Republican voters.

V

THE IMPACT OF THE MASS MEDIA

THE 1952 CAMPAIGN witnessed the dramatic diffusion of television as a major campaign forum. In Chapter II, "The Arena of Political Competition," it was seen that television exceeded both radio and the press as a chief source of public information about the presidential campaign. Because of its visual content, television was particularly well suited to create favorable images of the candidates. The availability of television for the first time in a presidential campaign was especially significant for the Democratic party. It helped widen the arena of competition and offered a likelihood of offsetting the advantage Republicans have traditionally enjoyed in the editorial outlook of the American press.

It should be recalled that the Republican party had a clear advantage in reaching their partisans through the mass media, although Republican partisans were fewer in numbers than Democratic partisans. Uncommitted citizens, having a generally lower involvement in politics than partisans of either party, were found to be least accessible through the mass news channels.

In general, there was no difference in the political objectives of Republicans and Democrats in their use of the mass media: first, to mobilize their partisan followers; second, to convert partisans from the opposition; and third, to attract doubtful citizens and nonvoters. However, for the Democratic party, the mass media had to help create a public image for a relatively unknown figure—Adlai Stevenson. Although the development of public imagery depends heavily upon casual conversation, the Democrats had to rely a great deal on the mass media to give favorable impetus to this process. The task of the Democrats was further complicated, since those voters who had to be mobilized as major sources of Democratic strength were rather harder to reach by radio, press, or television. The strategy of the Republicans was different in emphasis. Their candidate had the initial advantage of personal reputation and political imagery. These had to be maintained. At the same time, any over-identification of Eisenhower as a Republican had to be avoided, so as not to hinder appeals to uncommitted citizens and especially to Democratic partisans.

It is impossible to judge precisely which of the various objectives actually received greatest emphasis by the mass media strategists of either party. Both parties apparently believed that victory depended, above all, upon attracting the uncommitted citizens, whether those citizens had formerly been voters or nonvoters. In any case, the survey research data indicate that the Republican victory resulted primarily from outright conversion of many 1948 Truman voters, and secondarily from the advantage held by Republicans over Democrats in mobilizing their own partisans. Republican success in mobilizing 1948 nonvoters was a much smaller factor in the Eisenhower victory.

The analysis of mass media impact had to proceed by tracing the resolution of the 1948-1952 presidential vote in terms of the details of the electorate's exposure to the mass media. The questions employed in the second wave of interviews made it possible to chart exposure to the major media, and to ascertain especially those who were already making use of television. For these purposes two different aspects of media impact were investigated, as reported in Chapter II. First, media exposure was defined in terms of the number of channels a citizen made use of "to follow the campaign closely." Second, a measure of media involvement was constructed for classifying citizens into media fans, ordinary users, and nonusers, as far as campaign news was concerned. Members of the electorate were also classified with respect to their involvement with each of the specific mass media—press, radio, and television.[1]

THE STRUCTURE OF THE CAMPAIGN AUDIENCE

Rigid experimental designs were not felt to be appropriate for analyzing the consequences of communications in a national

[1]See Technical Appendix, Section 4, "Operational Definitions of Mass Media Exposure and Involvement," for the details of this measure.

election campaign. More appropriately, the impact of mass media exposure on voting behavior was seen as operating within the limits set by the structure of the campaign audience. The same variables used for analyzing presidential voting behavior seemed equally appropriate for delimiting the structure of the campaign audience. To be aware that the survey research methodology hardly permits "discovering" simple causal relations, does not relieve the social scientist of the responsibility of applying his theoretical constructs in order to infer patterns of influence.

The campaign audience was traced in terms of social structure, then in terms of social psychological predispositions, and finally in terms of political orientations. Selective controls were introduced when there appeared to be theoretical or empirical justifications.[2]

When analyzed in terms of social class, the patterns of media exposure highlight the problems facing the Democratic party in 1952. Low social class tends to be linked with limited educational level. Both of these attributes are relatively frequent among those segments of voters which are recognized as basic sources of Democratic support. Table XXII shows clearly that high mass media exposure to campaign information is related both to social class and to educational level. When level of education is held constant, the incidence of extensive media exposure rises progressively, class by class. And within each social class, higher educational level likewise implies greater exposure to the mass media.

More significant for inferring impact is the measure of involvement with specific media. When class patterns of involvement were examined, it became clear that television gave the Democrats a chance to counteract some of the traditional advantages

[2]To delimit the campaign audience in meaningful terms we had to recognize the contributions that might result from alternative patterns of analysis. This did not imply an exhaustive process of interrelating all variables in all possible patterns. Instead, the analysis of audience structure followed the lines pursued earlier in accounting for the patterns of presidential voting behavior. By using the same variables to analyze the structure of the campaign audience and the resolution of presidential voting patterns, it was felt that some inferences about the complex and interactive impact of the mass media might be drawn.

TABLE XXII

SOCIAL CLASS, MASS MEDIA EXPOSURE,
AND EDUCATIONAL LEVEL
(Per Cent)

	Upper-Middle	Lower-Middle	Upper-Lower	Lower-Lower	Farmers	Total†
FULLER EDUCA-TION*						
Followed Campaign						
Closely: on two or more media . . .	53.9	46.8	40.0	29.2	42.3	45.3
Closely: on one medium	27.7	29.4	33.1	36.7	28.9	30.6
Occasional exposure.	18.4	22.8	23.8	29.2	25.0	22.6
No media usage . .	0.0	1.0	3.1	4.9	3.8	1.6
Number	(217)	(201)	(160)	(41)	(52)	(671)
LIMITED EDUCA-TION‡						
Followed Campaign						
Closely: on two or more media . . .	39.1	27.8	34.2	14.7	20.1	25.4
Closely: on one medium.	32.7	35.7	29.2	28.9	27.8	30.1
Occasional exposure	26.0	31.7	32.4	38.7	41.0	35.2
No media usage	2.2	4.8	4.2	17.7	11.1	9.3
Number	(46)	(126)	(260)	(232)	(144)	(808)

*Education continued into or beyond high school.
†Total excludes 135 for which no basis for classification into social class was available.
‡Education did not continue into high school.

held by Republicans in the American press. In fact, television upset the simple formula that higher social class and educational level imply greater exposure to the mass media. When the middle class and the lower class were compared, the amount of television involvement in both classes was roughly equal.

Both in the middle class and in the lower class, television was the sole mass medium drawing nearly as great a concentration of fans (intense involvement) among those with limited education as among those with fuller education (see Table XXIII).

TABLE XXIII

MEDIA INVOLVEMENT, SOCIAL CLASS, AND EDUCATIONAL LEVEL
(Per Cent)

| | Middle Class | | Lower Class | | |
	Fuller Education	Limited Education	Fuller Education	Limited Education	Total*
Television fans....	82.7	76.6	74.0	67.9	74.7
Ordinary television users .	17.3	23.4	26.0	32.1	25.3
Number	(162)	(64)	(100)	(153)	(538)
Radio fans.......	80.2	65.3	71.8	55.9	64.0
Ordinary radio users	19.8	34.7	28.2	44.1	36.0
Number	(96)	(49)	(46)	(161)	(499)
Newspaper fans...	74.4	55.2	66.7	48.7	58.4
Ordinary newspaper users	25.6	44.8	33.3	51.3	41.6
Number	(117)	(47)	(42)	(115)	(403)

*Total includes 151 cases for which adequate social class and educational level data were not available.

Moreover, among those with limited education in both social classes, the incidence of television fans was greater than the incidence of newspaper or radio fans. Thus, in analyzing the impact of the mass media on voting behavior, the relationships cannot be thought of as reflecting only social class or educational differences.

As with social class, we may presume that psychological predispositions among voters predated patterns of mass media exposure to campaign efforts. In describing the structure of the campaign audience, it was important to learn whether those who relied most heavily on the mass media in general, or on a particular medium, tended to approach the campaign with low self-confidence. If this were the case, those who were most deeply involved would have the highest potentialities for being manipulated, since they would be the least likely to react with discrimination to the contents of the mass media.

TABLE XXIV

Mass Media Exposure and Psychological Predispositions
(Per Cent)

	Followed Campaign Closely on:				
	Two or More Media	One Medium	Occasional Exposure	No Usage	Total*
Political self-confidence					
High	74.2	55.6	42.3	22.1	56.0
Low	25.8	44.4	57.7	77.9	44.0
Self-interest in elections					
Strong	50.7	45.7	43.4	38.4	46.2
Weak	49.3	54.3	56.6	61.6	53.8
Number	(546)	(479)	(471)	(99)	(1,595)

*Total excludes nineteen cases for which no basis for classification was available.

Critics who stress the manipulative aspects of the mass media claim that the media attract mainly low political self-confidence members of the electorate who are more fascinated by the drama of the spectacle than helped in a deliberation of issues. These speculations were not confirmed by the data. Table XXIV indicates a positive relation between extensive mass media exposure and high political self-confidence. The desire to keep informed about the campaign and the drama of the campaign alike attracted those with high political self-confidence, whereas the group low in political self-confidence tended to avoid the mass media. Moreover, the finding that television, specifically, had more fans than any other medium cannot be attributed to its special attraction for those with low political self-confidence (see Table XXV). In fact, television attracted more fans with both high and low confidence than did either radio or the press, but still drew a higher proportion from the high-confidence than from the low-confidence group.

Thus, it appears that political predispositions tended to operate as "built-in" limitations on the manipulative potential of the mass media, and thus gave the competition a fuller chance to produce political consent. Furthermore, in the process of

TABLE XXV

POLITICAL SELF-CONFIDENCE AND MASS MEDIA INVOLVEMENT
(Per Cent)

	Political Self-confidence		
	High	Low	Total
Newspaper			
Fans	67.4	44.5	58.4
Ordinary users	32.6	55.5	41.6
Number	(243)	(160)	(403)
Radio			
Fans	72.1	55.1	64.0
Ordinary users	27.9	44.9	36.0
Number	(261)	(238)	(499)
Television			
Fans	79.9	66.3	74.7
Ordinary users	20.1	33.7	25.3
Number	(335)	(203)	(538)

deliberation the voter's estimate of the personal character of the candidates was revealed to be an important element. Television at least supplied a new basis for judgment—the personal appearance of the candidate.

As far as self-interest in elections was concerned, the expected association between high self-interest and extensive mass media exposure emerged (see Table XXIV). Self-selection was clearly at work. Although the association was present, it was not as marked as that between high political self-confidence and mass media exposure.

To complete the analysis, patterns of exposure to the mass media were classified in terms of ideological orientations and imagery of candidates (see Table XXVI and Table XXVII). As expected, there was a positive association between mass media involvement and explicit ideological orientation. The highest incidence of party stalwarts was found among fans; the lowest incidence among nonusers. The same was true of party compromisers, but the reverse pattern emerged for weak party

TABLE XXVI

MASS MEDIA INVOLVEMENT AND IDEOLOGICAL ORIENTATIONS
(Per Cent)

	Fans	Ordinary Users	Non-users	Total*
Party stalwarts...........	18.9	8.8	4.8	15.6
Party compromisers........	35.6	27.6	18.3	31.4
Weak party compromisers..	27.1	42.4	57.7	34.0
Ambivalents or neutrals	18.4	21.2	19.2	19.0
Number	(957)	(485)	(104)	(1,614)

*Total column includes 137 cases for which breakdown by mass media involvement is not available.

compromisers. However, the incidence of those with ambivalent-neutral ideological orientations was roughly the same (about 20 per cent) among mass media fans, ordinary users, and non-users. Here, too, it appears that audience-imposed limitations on the manipulative consequences of the mass media were at work, as far as campaign issues were concerned.

By contrast, imagery of either candidate seemed more closely associated with involvement with the mass media, but in a somewhat complex fashion. Audience-imposed limitations operated to the extent that strong candidate preferences were equally manifested without regard to involvement in the mass media. On the other hand, the consequences of high involvement could be inferred among those who held weak candidate preferences. The concentration of citizens with either mild or ambivalent

TABLE XXVII

MASS MEDIA INVOLVEMENT AND CANDIDATE IMAGERY PREFERENCES
(Per Cent)

	Fans	Ordinary Users	Non-users
Strong candidate preference..........	42.7	44.6	43.3
Mild candidate preference............	30.2	21.4	6.7
Ambivalent candidate imagery........	21.0	17.5	11.5
No image of candidate...............	6.1	16.5	38.5
Number	(957)	(485)	(104)

TABLE XXVIII

Mass Media Involvement and the 1952 Presidential Vote

(Per Cent)

	Media Fans			Ordinary Users			Nonusers	Total*
	Tele-vision	News-papers	Radio	Tele-vision	News-papers	Radio		
Eisenhower voters	48.1	55.7	47.2	30.9	35.1	32.4	12.5	42.5
Stevenson voters	38.8	32.4	28.4	37.5	32.2	21.4	16.3	30.6
Nonvoters	11.9	11.9	24.1	30.2	30.3	45.6	69.3	26.0
Other or not ascertained..	1.2	0.0	0.3	1.4	2.4	0.6	1.9	0.9
Number	(402)	(234)	(321)	(136)	(168)	(182)	(104)	(1,614)

*Total column includes 137 cases for which no breakdown can be shown.

candidate imagery was heaviest among those with high levels of involvement; conversely, those with no clear imagery tended to have lower levels of involvement. Thus, strong identification with either candidate represented more than impressions derived from the mass media, whereas weaker identifications were more likely to be conditioned by the media.

EXPOSURE, INVOLVEMENT, AND THE RESOLUTION OF THE VOTE

The next step in analyzing the impact of the mass media was to classify the campaign audience by voting patterns. As stated above, the underlying assumption was that the mass media were interactive with the key variables used in analyzing voting behavior. No simple relationships were likely to emerge, but influence patterns might be inferred.

Indirectly, the data could help answer three important questions. First, did the mass media stimulate voting through activation of nonvoters, and if so, could the increase be linked specifically to exposure to television, press, or radio? Second, did the mass media help Republicans more than Democrats in mobilizing their partisans? And third, did television play a special role in the resolution of the final vote?

First there is the role of the mass media in activating nonvoters to go to the polls: the data show than the incidence of nonvoting in 1952 was inversely and markedly related to mass media involvement (see Table XXVIII). The extraordinarily high concentration of nonvoting among nonusers of the mass media was 69.3 per cent. Although 35.7 per cent of the ordinary media users failed to vote, only 16.1 per cent of the media fans were nonvoters. These data underline the extent of the interactive pattern between media involvement and voting.

Nonvoting was substantially less frequent among the television fans than among ordinary users of television. A heavy involvement with the press had the same marked consequences. Among radio listeners the level of involvement was also inversely related to nonvoting, but less markedly so. Since none of these differences seem likely to be explained by social class or educa-

TABLE XXIX

MASS MEDIA INVOLVEMENT AND VOTING PATTERNS, 1948-1952
(Per Cent)

1948-1952 Vote	Media Fans	Ordinary Users	Non-users	Total*
Regular party voters.........	56.5	41.5	11.2	48.7
Voting changers	32.0	27.9	28.6	30.5
Persistent nonvoters..........	11.5	31.7	60.2	20.8
Number	(877)	(441)	(98)	(1,416)

*Total excludes 198 cases for which no basis for classification was available.

tional level alone, the data not only link voting to mass media exposure but also indicate the differential consequences of high involvement with television, radio, and the press.

Analysis of persistent nonvoting from 1948 to 1952 only duplicates these findings. Among nonusers, 60.2 per cent were persistent nonvoters, compared with 28.6 per cent among media users and 11.2 per cent among fans (see Table XXIX). In addition, more refined analysis of these data than presented in this table reveals that the pattern of exposure of the 1948 voters who became nonvoters in 1952—the "drop-outs"—was similar to that of persistent nonvoters. Contrariwise, the 1948 nonvoters who were mobilized in 1952, either by the Republicans or by the Democrats, had a level of mass media involvement approaching that of the regular party voters.

Still other data highlight the differential association between persistent nonvoting and exposure to specific mass media. Although there was a similar incidence of persistent nonvoters in the television and press audience (11.0 and 12.9 per cent respectively), the incidence of persistent nonvoters in the radio audience reached 25.9 per cent (see Table XXX).

The second question to be answered was: Did the mass media help Republicans more than Democrats in mobilizing their partisans? The Republican partisans who voted for Eisenhower included a higher concentration of mass media fans than did Democratic partisans who voted for Stevenson (89.4 per cent among the Republican partisans and 58.8 per cent among the

TABLE XXX
MASS MEDIA EXPOSURE AND VOTING PATTERNS, 1948-1952
(Per Cent)

	Mass Media Audience			Non-users	Total*
	Tele-vision	Press	Radio		
Regular party voters.......	57.2	54.7	45.7	11.8	48.5
Voting changers	31.8	32.4	28.4	30.1	31.2
Persistent nonvoters	11.0	12.9	25.9	58.1	20.3
Number	(514)	(390)	(469)	(93)	(1,446)
Pattern Breakdown Regular party voters:					
Republicans..........	48.8	50.0	55.8	....	....
Democrats	51.2	50.0	44.2	....	....
Number	(293)	(208)	(219)	(11)†	....
Voting changers:					
Pro-Eisenhower	65.3	78.8	73.7	64.3	....
Pro-Stevenson	34.7	21.2	26.3	35.7	....
Number	(164)	(123)	(133)	(28)	....

*Total excludes 168 cases for which no basis for classification was available.
†Too few cases for statistical analysis.

Democratic ones (see Table XXXI). These data not only reflect the initially greater involvement of Republican partisans in the mass media as compared with Democratic partisans. They also support the inference that the mass media helped the Republicans to mobilize their partisans to a greater extent than the Democrats.

Among both Republican and Democratic partisans, nonvoting declined as media involvement increased. Correspondingly, as media involvement increased, the vote increased for Eisenhower and for Stevenson (see Table XXXI). However, the increase in Eisenhower voters among the Republican partisans was twice as great proportionately as the increase in Stevenson voters among the Democratic partisans. Moreover, among Democratic partisans, the decline in nonvoting associated with intensive mass media exposure augmented the Eisenhower vote to some degree as well. Intensive mass media expo-

TABLE XXXI
MASS MEDIA INVOLVEMENT AND THE 1952 PRESIDENTIAL VOTE
(PER CENT)

	Fans	Ordinary Users	Nonusers	Total*
Republican Partisans				
Eisenhower voters	89.4	68.9	....	82.1
Stevenson voters	2.5	2.7	....	2.5
Nonvoters	8.1	28.4	....	13.2
Other and not ascertained	0.0	0.0	....	2.2
Number	(236)	(74)	(10)†	(325)
Uncommitted Electors				
Eisenhower voters	54.3	33.3	11.9	41.8
Stevenson voters.........	24.7	19.3	10.1	22.9
Nonvoters	19.8	44.8	78.0	30.4
Other and not ascertained	1.2	2.6	0.0	4.9
Number	(341)	(228)	(59)	(655)
Democratic Partisans				
Eisenhower voters	22.7	16.2	8.6	20.0
Stevenson voters	58.8	48.0	31.4	50.0
Nonvoters	18.2	35.3	60.0	25.6
Other and not ascertained	6.3	0.5	0.0	4.4
Number	(362)	(204)	(35)	(634)

*Total includes sixty-five cases for which mass media involvement was not ascertained.
†Too few cases for statistical analysis.

sure for the uncommitted electorate was associated with a higher proportion of Eisenhower than Stevenson voters.

The third question to be answered was: Did television play a special role in the resolution of the final vote? Is there any basis for the contention that television, by dramatizing a relatively unknown standard bearer, tended to prevent even more defection than occurred from the Democratic bloc?

Toward the end of the campaign, when the first wave of interviews was being carried out, it was possible to gauge voters' expectations as to who would win the election. Since these interviews were collected mainly in October, 1952, much of the effort to dramatize the candidates by means of the mass media had already taken place. Expectations about victory varied widely and they were related to the medium which the individual reported was most important for him as a source of political campaign news. Within the limits inherent in drawing inferences about complex interactive relationships, the role of television began to emerge.

The television audience had the most balanced estimates, with 46.9 per cent believing in an Eisenhower victory and 41.4 per cent believing in a Stevenson victory. By contrast, 65.5 per cent of the newspaper audience expected Eisenhower to win, whereas the percentage dropped precipitously to 16.1 per cent for an expected Stevenson victory. Part of the explanation lies in the self-selection of a medium by the audience, since newspapers were the least neutral in their over-all presentation. By contrast, television was probably the most balanced. However, in the light of all that has been said about the characteristics of the mass media audience, self-selection alone does not seem to account for all these differences.

Additional inferences about the impact of television can be drawn from an examination of mass media exposure and the various patterns of 1948-1952 voting behavior. As a group, the changers displayed equal incidence of exposure to television, newspapers, and radio (approximately one-third of the audience for these three media were changers; see Table XXX).

However, when the changers were classified as pro-Eisenhower and pro-Stevenson, a statistically significant difference in media exposure emerged (see Table XXXII). The incidence of television exposure among regular Democratic voters (41.1 per cent) was equal to that of the pro-Stevenson changers (43.0 per cent). However, the incidence for pro-Stevenson changers was statistically higher than the incidence for pro-Eisenhower changers (31.5 per cent). The incidence among regular Republican voters (37.2 per cent) did not reach that of either Democratic voting group. Thus, since higher levels of television exposure were linked to voting patterns tending to be favorable to the Democrats—regular voters and pro-Democratic changers—it does appear that, at the least, television exposure probably prevented an even worse Democratic result.

TABLE XXXII

VOTING PATTERNS, 1948-1952, AND MASS MEDIA EXPOSURE
(Per Cent)

	Regular Republican Voters	Regular Democratic Voters	Pro-Eisenhower Ch'ngrs	Pro-Stevenson Ch'ngrs	Persistent Nonvoters	Total*
Media Exposure:						
Television	37.2	41.1	31.5	43.0	42.2	33.5
Radio	28.8	26.2	28.6	24.8	42.2	30.5
Newspapers ...	27.2	28.8	28.3	18.2	17.1	24.9
Nonusers	0.5	2.5	5.2	7.3	18.2	6.3
Not ascertained	11.1	5.2	10.2	9.5	7.3	8.6
Number	(386)	(365)	(343)	(137)	(315)	(1,546)

*Total excludes sixty-eight cases for which voting pattern was not ascertained. Columns do not add to 100 per cent because a few persons followed the campaign on more than one medium.

Conversely, whereas regular Republican voters, regular Democratic voters, and pro-Republican changers had approximately the same incidence of press exposure (27.2 per cent, 28.8 per cent, and 28.3 per cent respectively), the incidence among pro-Democratic changers dropped markedly to 18.2 per cent. Finally, no patterns linking voting change to radio listening could be discerned, since all voting segments revealed equal levels of radio exposure.

At this point, further analysis of the impact of the mass media is premature. It is necessary to include in the analysis political party and primary group pressures which supplied the mediating context for the mass media.

VI

INTERPERSONAL AND ORGANIZATIONAL PRESSURES

IN THE ANALYSIS of campaign pressures, television, radio, and the newspapers were seen as the mass vehicles by which political arguments and candidate imagery were brought into the daily life of the voting population. In a diverse and complex society, the mass media of communications had the indispensable task of giving the American electorate a common ground for political discussion. They emphasized for voters the central and nation-wide importance of a few issues; they dramatized the contest between two men, Eisenhower and Stevenson. Thus, despite regional and community differences in emphasis, the 1952 presidential campaign developed a common thematic meaning throughout the nation.

In every community some citizens were relatively untouched by the campaign of 1952, whereas others were actively engaged in persuading daily associates how to vote, in giving money, in attending political rallies, or in working on behalf of a candidate or a party. The sampled electorate was asked a series of questions about personal political participation. Roughly one out of every three persons qualified as having been an "active citizen"—a participant in at least one of these campaign activities in his community. This ratio was found to prevail in all types of political communities except southern Democratic strongholds, where only one out of four were active citizens (see Table XXXIII).

No national election can qualify as a genuine "process of consent" rather than be an act of mass manipulation unless it includes widespread interaction and opinion formation at the community level. The values that guide political action are not exclusively those coming from membership in functional organizations, such as labor unions, business associations, or farm groups. Mediating between the individual and the cor-

TABLE XXXIII
GEOGRAPHICAL STRONGHOLDS AND CAMPAIGN PARTICIPATION
(Per Cent)

	Republican Strongholds	Competitive Areas	Democratic Strongholds		Total Electorate
			Northern	Southern	
Active citizens........	30.2	33.5	31.6	26.3	31.2
Passive citizens	69.8	66.5	68.4	73.7	68.8
Number	(304)	(653)	(323)	(334)	(1,614)

porate life of society are primary group associations—friends, co-workers, family—which demand a person's loyalty and own much of his allegiance. Since people "talked politics" extensively at work, with their friends, and in the privacy of their families, these conversations mediated between the citizen and the mass media. Together with local canvassing, the flow of interpersonal pressures could be assumed to have had a meaningful influence on voting behavior. The American voter, then, could hardly be thought of as an isolated individual, a random member of a mass society who was easy prey to direct pressure from the mass media.

We thus arrive at the fourth and fifth preconditions for a competitive election to qualify as a process of consent. The quality of an election depends upon the extent to which limitations operate to prevent the means of mass communications and the organized techniques of persuasion from exercising monopolization or even pervasive influence by one party. Thus, the question arises: How pervasive were the political pressures exerted by primary group relationships, and did they support or counteract the influence of the mass media in determining voting behavior?

INFORMAL POLITICAL INTERACTION

To assess the quality of politics in a democratic competition, critical note must be taken of how concentrated partisans are among active citizens in the various geographic strongholds. Central issues and candidate imagery, brought into the community setting by the mass media, seem more apt to get thoughtful consideration if both the Republican and Democratic viewpoints are supported by substantial numbers of the active citizens in the locality. If, for example, virtually all active citizens tended to be spokesmen for the Republican cause, those who were essentially passive about politics would tend to get a one-sided version of issues from the more politically active citizens. There would remain for them the stylized, carefully calculated set of campaign appeals available through television, radio, or the press. In a very real sense, the Democratic version would become only a formal alternative for them, one apparently not taken seriously by the more active citizens. For many such passive citizens, those conditions would be missing that make elections a meaningful process of consent in which they take part.

Table XXXIV shows that for any type of geographic stronghold it may be inferred that the passive citizens were aware of a respectable minority of political actives championing the Democratic position. These data support and amplify the previous observation (see Table I) that there was widespread doubt about the outcome of the election. They also underline once more the extensive level of political competition for the nation as a whole in 1952. In Republican strongholds, and even in the Northern Democratic strongholds, those actively participating in the campaign were in the ratio of two Eisenhower adherents to every one for Stevenson. Such a ratio could be considered as meeting basic competitive requirements, since there was no area where one party's active participants dominated the scene overwhelmingly. In the southern Democratic strongholds, active Stevenson adherents were in a one-to-one ratio with Eisenhower adherents, an even more competitive balance.[1]

[1]Further examination of Table XXXIV reveals an additional point of interest. In the most entrenched positions of either party—the Republican strongholds and southern Democratic strongholds—the ratio of Eisenhower to Stevenson voters among passive citizens was not significantly different from the ratio among the

TABLE XXXIV

CITIZEN PARTICIPATION, GEOGRAPHICAL STRONGHOLDS,
AND THE 1952 VOTE
(Per Cent)

	Active Citizens (Ratio)	Passive Citizens (Ratio)
Republican Strongholds:		
Eisenhower voters	67.1	71.1
Stevenson voters	32.9	28.9
Number	(88)	(169)
Competitive Areas:		
Eisenhower voters	65.8	54.8
Stevenson voters	34.2	45.2
Number	(196)	(303)
Northern Democratic Strongholds:		
Eisenhower voters	63.8	44.5
Stevenson voters	36.2	55.5
Number	(94)	(169)
Southern Democratic Strongholds:		
Eisenhower voters	50.0	47.1
Stevenson voters	50.0	52.9
Number	(60)	(102)
TOTAL ELECTORATE		
Eisenhower voters	63.4	55.1
Stevenson voters	36.6	44.9
Number	(438)	(743)

more active citizens. However, in the more doubtful areas, these ratios were significantly different. In the northern Democratic strongholds, as well as in the "competitive areas," the ratio of Eisenhower to Stevenson voters among passive citizens was about one to one, whereas among active citizens the ratio was roughly two to one. Perhaps in these more politically doubtful localities, informal political leadership is a more complex phenomenon than elsewhere; probably the dramatic alternatives of the election were made meaningful to the passive citizens through a wider range of campaign pressures. In any event, it is clear that the voting behavior of active citizens in these relatively doubtful areas did not provide, in 1952, any safe basis for predicting how close the contest would be among the "silent voters."

A more direct measure of the patterns of interpersonal pressure lies in the concerted nature of primary group pressures on the voter. It seems doubtful that extensive use of the mass media, by itself, could have recruited for Eisenhower so many new Republican voters and at the same time retained so many regular Republican voters. What part, then, was played by the casually registered primary group pressure of daily associates who were concertedly pro-Eisenhower?

After the election, people in the national sample were asked how their friends, co-workers, and family had voted. From the answers they gave, it was possible to isolate those who were subject to concerted primary group pressures in one direction—those who reported that friends, family, and co-workers had all voted the same way. Far more members of the electorate were subject to concerted primary group pressure in favor of Eisenhower than of Stevenson, despite the preponderance of Democratic partisans in the population: 21.7 per cent of the electorate were under concertedly pro-Eisenhower pressure, whereas 10.7 per cent were under concertedly pro-Stevenson pressure. As was expected, the bulk of the electorate—the remaining two-thirds—was under conflicting or neutralized pressures from daily associates.

Table **XXXV** indicates the strong conditioning effects on voting behavior of concerted pressure by daily associates. Self reported primary group pressure is a complex and interactive variable; nevertheless the fact emerged that pro-Stevenson pressure was linked to a 78.1 per cent Stevenson vote and pro-Eisenhower pressure was even more closely linked to voting, resulting in votes for Eisenhower 88.5 per cent of the time.

CANVASSING BY RIVAL PARTIES

The major political parties of the United States are based on their local organizations, which in campaign years do extensive canvassing. The effects of party canvassing on American voting behavior are comparatively unknown. Shortly after the election those in the national sample of the electorate were asked whether

TABLE XXXV

PRIMARY GROUP PRESSURES AND THE 1952 PRESIDENTIAL VOTE
(Per Cent)

	Concerted Pro-Eisenhower Pressure	Conflicting or Neutral-ized Pressure	Concerted Pro-Stevenson Pressure
Eisenhower voters	88.5	35.3	2.3
Stevenson voters ...	4.6	32.5	78.1
Nonvoters	6.9	32.2	19.6
Number	(322)	(1,021)	(166)

they had been contacted during the campaign by party workers, and if so, by which party.[2] "Canvassing" here meant attempts at persuasion by local fellow citizens acting as spokesmen for the major parties. As reported in Chapter II, approximately 12.3 per cent of the electorate, or at least six million households, were contacted by canvassers for one or both parties. Moreover, it appears that Republican workers reached as many, if not more, potential voters than did the Democrats.

The scope of party canvassing in 1952 emerged from a three-way comparison of those canvassed by Republicans, those canvassed by Democrats, and those not canvassed (see Table XXXVI). On nine separate characteristics, canvassing by both parties reached much the same types of citizens. Each party did seem to have concentrated in the competitive areas, while they seem to have done less canvassing in southern Democratic strongholds. Republican and Democratic canvassing efforts were similar in their social class and ethnic-religious group incidence. Both parties tended to slight the lower-lower class and, to a statistically significant degree, devoted disproportionate efforts among the ethnic-religious minorities—Catholics, Jews, and Negroes. Both also reached a cross section of voters in terms of partisanship, candidate imagery, and primary group pressure.

On three of the nine characteristics, however, although no important differences between Republican and Democratic

[2] " . . . Did anybody from either one of the parties call you up or come around and talk to you during the campaign?"

TABLE XXXVI
THE INCIDENCE OF PARTY CANVASSING IN 1952
(Per Cent)

	Canvassed by Republicans	Canvassed by Democrats	Not Canvassed
Republican strongholds	16.1	14.5	19.4
Competitive areas	50.0	52.8	38.1
Northern Democratic strongholds	21.0	19.1	20.8
Southern Democratic strongholds....	12.9	13.6	21.7
Upper-middle class	21.8	20.0	15.8
Lower middle class................	23.4	25.5	20.0
Upper-lower class.................	32.3	29.1	25.4
Lower-lower class.................	6.4	11.8	17.7
Farmers and others................	16.1	13.6	21.1
Protestants (white)	58.8	54.5	67.5
Ethnic-religious minorities	41.2	45.5	32.5
Republican partisans	23.2	18.0	19.8
Uncommitted electorate	38.4	40.5	40.7
Democratic partisans	38.4	41.5	39.5
Pro-Republican imagery............	32.5	29.6	29.6
Ambivalent or neutral imagery	31.7	25.9	34.7
Pro-Democratic imagery	35.8	44.5	35.7
High political self-confidence........	68.6	66.5	54.2
Low political self-confidence........	31.4	33.5	45.8
Strong self-interest in elections.......	51.6	55.6	45.1
Weak self-interest in elections........	48.4	44.4	54.9
Active citizens	55.9	53.6	28.3
Passive citizens	44.1	46.4	71.7
Concerted pro-Eisenhower pressure...	28.4	21.1	21.2
Conflicting or neutralized pressure....	58.6	66.1	68.5
Concerted pro-Stevenson pressure	13.0	12.8	10.3
Number	(124)	(110)	(1,417)

canvassing efforts were found, those who were canvassed differed to a statistically significant degree from those not canvassed. Those who were canvassed included a greater concentration of persons with high political self-confidence, strong self-interest in elections, and a record of having been active in the campaign. These types may have been more prominent on party canvassing lists than the non-canvassed electorate. Moreover, they were types whose political predisposition or campaign behavior made it likely that they would vote in a presidential election whether canvassed or not.

For the national electorate as a whole, party canvassing apparently had the effect of "activating" a substantial number who might otherwise have failed to vote. Among those not canvassed, 27.9 per cent were nonvoters in 1952; among canvassed persons, only 12.7 per cent did not vote. But it is possible that canvassing was consciously directed toward persons who would in any case have been more likely to vote. To the extent that this was true, the activation effect was inefficient.

To investigate this more closely, a comparison was made of the incidence of nonvoting among canvassed and noncanvassed portions of the various segments of the electorate (see Table XXXVII). The basic finding was that the activation effect was present for all nine characteristics investigated—that is, when comparisons were made in terms of geographic locale, social class, ethnic-religious grouping, political partisanship, party imagery, political self-confidence, self-interest in elections, active citizenship, and primary group pressures. To be sure, the activation effect of canvassing was rather unimportant for some characteristics. In particular, the tendency for both major parties to canvass heavily among "active citizens" may have been inefficient in 1952, because it was a waste of effort to canvass persons who, in a *presidential* election, would almost certainly vote. But one must be cautious in applying these findings for 1952 to campaigns in which other political pressures are far less intensive and in which the role of the party canvass may well be more critical.

After his activation, how the canvassed voter cast his ballot was a different matter, by no means in direct consequence of having been canvassed by Democrats or Republicans. By activating more voters, the canvassers may have helped their party, but they could not expect to be perfect salesmen. By

TABLE XXXVII

Party Canvassing and the Incidence of Nonvoting in 1952
(Per Cent)

	Incidence of Nonvoting		
	Canvassed by One or Both Parties	Not Canvassed	Direction of Incidence*
Republican strongholds...............	0.0	15.9	+
Competitive areas	14.0	24.8	+
Northern Democratic strongholds	11.1	18.2	+
Southern Democratic strongholds.......	21.4	54.5	+
Upper-middle class	0.0	12.1	+
Lower-middle class..................	11.4	19.8	+
Upper-lower class...................	16.7	24.4	+
Lower-lower class	18.5	46.8	+
Protestants (white)..................	13.3	24.8	+
Ethnic-religious minorities............	9.9	31.7	+
Republican partisans	11.4	13.8	+
Uncommitted electorate .....·........	11.4	34.4	+
Democratic partisans	16.6	31.8	+
Pro-Republican imagery..............	9.5	15.3	+
Ambivalent or neutral imagery	8.7	23.9	+
Pro-Democratic imagery	13.7	31.0	+
High political self-confidence	8.6	17.5	+
Low political self-confidence...........	20.3	39.8	+
Strong self-interest in elections........	11.9	27.9	+
Weak self-interest in elections.........	13.5	27.4	+
Active citizens......................	10.8	12.5	+
Passive citizens	14.9	33.8	+
Concerted pro-Eisenhower pressure....	4.0	7.5	+
Conflicting or neutralized pressure.....	16.8	34.9	+
Concerted pro-Stevenson pressure	9.1	20.8	+
National electorate..................	12.7	27.9	+
Number	(196)	(1,417)	

*Plus sign (+) indicates greater incidence among noncanvassed as compared with canvassed; minus (−) indicates the converse.

TABLE XXXVIII
Party Canvassing and the Incidence of Presidential Voters
(Per Cent)

	Canvassed by Republicans: Per Cent of Eisenhower Voters*	Not Canvassed: Ratio of Eisenhower to Stevenson Voters		Canvassed by Democrats: Per Cent of Stevenson Voters†
		Eisenhower	Stevenson	
Republican strongholds and competitive areas	59.7	69.2	30.8	43.7
Northern and southern Demo. strongholds ..	51.3	49.8	50.2	50.0
Middle class	67.3	68.7	31.3	37.8
Lower class..........	42.5	44.4	55.6	63.9
Protestants (white)	67.7	66.3	33.7	32.3
Ethnic-religious minorities	43.8	42.3	57.7	62.0
Republican partisans...	92.8	97.6	2.4	0.0
Uncommitted electorate	64.1	66.4	33.6	63.9
Democratic partisans...	33.3	27.3	72.7	55.3
Pro-Republican imagery	86.1	96.9	3.1	12.9
Ambivalent or neutral imagery	74.3	62.2	37.8	33.3
Pro-Democratic imagery	18.4	15.7	84.3	84.6
High political self-confidence..........	57.7	59.4	40.6	46.2
Low political self-confidence..........	51.9	57.1	42.9	51.7
Strong self-interest in elections	53.6	55.0	45.0	48.1
Weak self-interest in elections	64.2	61.6	38.4	47.6
Active citizens	54.7	65.6	34.4	44.2
Passive citizens........	64.4	55.8	44.2	52.3
Concerted pro-Eisenhower pressure......	93.9	95.5	4.5	9.1
Conflicting or neutralized pressure........	53.2	52.1	47.9	51.7
Concerted pro-Stevenson pressure	0.0	3.5	96.5	100.0
National electorate	58.7	58.8	41.2	47.9

*Based on a ratio of Eisenhower votes to Stevenson votes.
†Based on a ratio of Stevenson votes to Eisenhower votes.

activating more voters than they could persuade to vote for their candidate, the workers of each party helped the cause of the rival party. After comparing the ratio of Eisenhower to Stevenson voters among noncanvassed persons with the corresponding ratios among those canvassed, we were able to make inferences about the effectiveness of the personal canvass. For a specific characteristic of the electorate when those canvassed divided at the polls in a ratio more favorable to one candidate than that prevailing among noncanvassed, it could be inferred that the canvassing was efficient, that is, worthwhile from the point of view of the party.

Table XXXVIII shows that the Republican canvass was rather inefficient in that it did not concentrate on those groups most likely to be influenced by the doorbell ringer. Only two characteristics were associated with successful Republican canvassing: passive citizenship and ambivalent or neutral imagery of the Republican party. However, the incidence of passive citizens canvassed was disproportionately low (see Table XXXVI). Presumably, those citizens were not readily identifiable by any visible group characteristics and were accessible only to the degree that the party organization had intimate and detailed knowledge of the local community.

By contrast, on seven of the nine major characteristics used in classifying the electorate, a comparison between those canvassed by Republicans and those not canvassed revealed virtually no improvement in the ratio of Eisenhower to Stevenson voters among the canvassed portion.

A similar analysis of the effects of Democratic canvassing is possible (see Table XXXVIII). There are some indications that Democratic canvassers were more persuasive than their Republican counterparts—notably in the results obtained in Republican strongholds and competitive areas, and particularly among the uncommitted electorate. In addition, there was similar but less marked improvement among the lower class and among ethnic-religious minority groups, low self-confidence groups, weak self-interest groups, and passive citizen groups. But the inefficiency of Democratic canvassing efforts is also documented by the time wasted, with little effect, among Republican partisans, persons with pro-Republican party imagery, and persons under concerted pro-Eisenhower pressure from their daily associates.

THE INTERPLAY OF CAMPAIGN PRESSURES

Thus far, campaign pressures have been considered individually. The process of consent is enhanced, it was argued, when the electorate is confronted with organized competition. But what can be learned about the interplay of significant campaign pressures—those from primary groups and the mass media of communications? One-third of the electorate was subject to concerted pressure by daily associates on behalf of one of the candidates. Did the political climate in which these men and women found themselves isolate them from the political competition generated by the mass media? Did primary group pressures give them a context for bolstering their basic convictions and thus help contain the manipulative impact of the campaign?

The data indicate that intense mass media involvement actually reinforced the concerted primary group pressures on individual voters (see Table XXXIX). First, those subject to concerted pressure from friends, co-workers, and family members seemed to expose themselves more to campaign rhetoric and imagery in the mass media than did those whose daily associates were divided in political preference: 62.3 per cent among the former were mass media fans, as against 53.2 per cent among the latter. Second, for those individuals who were subject to concerted primary group pressures—pro-Eisenhower or pro-Stevenson—a higher incidence of voting could be found among fans than among ordinary users of the mass media. Moreover, the increased voting among mass media fans was overwhelmingly in the direction of the concerted primary group pressure.

Concerted primary group pressure can hardly be said, therefore, to insulate the citizen from the impact of the mass media. On the contrary, it seems to have reinforced the mass media in conditioning higher levels of voting. But the question that remains unanswered by the data relates to the deliberative

TABLE XXXIX

PRIMARY GROUP PRESSURES, MASS MEDIA INVOLVEMENT,
AND THE 1952 PRESIDENTIAL VOTE
(Per Cent)

	Primary Group Pressures*		
	Concerted Pro-Eisenhower	Conflicting or Neutral	Concerted Pro-Stevenson
Mass Media Fans:			
Eisenhower voters......	94.1	40.4	7.9
Stevenson voters.......	2.1	37.7	82.3
Nonvoters	3.8	21.9	9.8
Number	(240)	(596)	(102)
Ordinary Users:			
Eisenhower voters......	77.0	28.4	3.7
Stevenson voters.......	12.8	29.6	66.7
Nonvoters	10.2	42.0	29.6
Number	(78)	(338)	(54)
Nonusers:			
Eisenhower voters......	....	10.4	....
Stevenson voters	....	13.8	....
Nonvoters	....	75.8	....
Number	(4)†	(87)	(10)†

*From family, friends, and co-workers.
†Too few cases for statistical analysis.

character of this voting. Since the mass media reinforced the aims of the concerted primary group pressures in the overwhelming majority of instances, they would seem to have encouraged conformity with the preferences of acquaintances rather than to have fostered effective deliberation.

However, for those under conflicting primary group pressures, the mass media operated as vehicles for transmitting the full range of competitive forces in the campaign. Neither party was outstandingly successful in its mass media appeals either to media fans or to ordinary users whose daily associates disagreed politically. Each party received about half of the votes cast by such members of the electorate (see Table XXXIX). Since they were not under concerted one-sided pressure from

TABLE XL

PRIMARY GROUP PRESSURES, MASS MEDIA INVOLVEMENT,
AND THE 1952 PRESIDENTIAL VOTE

	Concerted Pro-Eisenhower (Per Cent)	Conflicting or Neutral (Per Cent)	Concerted Pro-Stevenson (Per Cent)	Total	
				Per Cent	Number
Newspaper Fans	27.8...	...61.9...	...10.3...	100.0	(233)
Eisenhower voters...	93.8	47.2	4.1		
Stevenson voters	3.6	35.4	91.8		
Nonvoters	2.6	17.4	4.1		
Number	(65)	(144)	(24)		
Television Fans	25.9...	...63.5...	...10.6...	100.0	(395)
Eisenhower voters...	95.1	38.0	7.1		
Stevenson voters	2.0	45.4	85.8		
Nonvoters	2.9	16.6	7.1		
Number	(102)	(251)	(42)		
Radio Fans	23.6...	...64.8...	...11.6...	100.0	(310)
Eisenhower voters...	93.1	38.8	11.1		
Stevenson voters	1.4	29.4	72.2		
Nonvoters	5.5	31.8	16.7		
Number	(73)	(201)	(36)		

daily associates to conform—a pressure shown to be extremely effective—these persons were potentially more independent and more skeptical. Perhaps they were also more indifferent to the arguments and imagery advanced by either side through the mass media. From the point of view of campaign managers, the uncertainty of the reaction from this large segment of the electorate probably resulted in a stressing of traditional political themes and images and a tendency to keep the competitive struggle within accepted limits.

Because television developed into the medium with the widest audience in the 1952 campaign, it was necessary to examine the interaction of this particular medium with primary group pressures (see Table XL). Among mass media fans who voted and were subject to concerted primary group pressures, television viewing proved to be very much like radio or newspaper exposure; most such persons conformed to the political consensus of their associates. However, 45.4 per cent of the television fans who were *not* subject to concerted primary group pressure gave Stevenson their votes. The comparable figures among radio and newspaper fans were 29.4 and 35.4 per cent. In short, television did provide a vehicle for the relatively unknown Democratic candidate to bring before those who actively followed the campaign his version of the issues and his personal qualifications. But it should be noted that Stevenson got almost no backing from television fans who were subject to concerted pro-Eisenhower pressures from daily associates.

Finally, among those subject to conflicting group pressure, what was the significance of social psychological predispositions in conditioning the impact of Eisenhower's and Stevenson's mass media appeal? Did either man's mass media campaign register marked success among the effective citizens, the indifferent citizens, or the involved spectators and apathetic persons? Three general patterns appeared.

First, in five out of six segments of the mass media audience not subject to concerted primary group pressures, Stevenson's appeals could be inferred as more persuasive than Republican strategy among effective citizens—that is, those who displayed both strong feelings of self-interest in the election outcome and high political self-confidence (see Table XLI). This was especially the case among effective citizens who were television fans. It suggests that Stevenson's attempt to portray himself as "the candidate who talks sense to the American people" was an appropriate strategy for that kind of an audience, and through that medium in particular.

Second, Eisenhower's appeals in the mass media were consistently linked to a disproportionate share of those who were highly self-confident but lacked a feeling of self-interest in the election outcome—the indifferent citizens. The tone of his campaign, his decision to barnstorm the country and the dramatization of his "crusade" were especially effective in mobilizing support from these indifferent citizens. The indifferent citizen's high political

TABLE XLI

Mass Media Involvement, Political Predispositions, and the 1952 Presidential Vote*

(Per Cent)

	Electorate Under Conflicting or Neutralized Primary Group Pressures					
	Media Fans			Ordinary Users		
	Television	Newspapers	Radio	Television	Newspapers	Radio
PROPORTION OF ELECTORAL BLOC WHO WERE:						
Effective citizens Stevenson voters	42.1	43.2	39.0	25.0	15.3	27.6
Rest of electorate	v 30.7	v 31.2	v 28.2	v 14.8	ʌ 17.1	v 20.7
Indifferent citizens Eisenhower voters	33.7	47.1	30.8	48.1	34.4	21.6
Rest of electorate	v 27.6	v 23.7	v 21.2	v 25.8	v 25.3	v 15.0
Involved spectators and apathetic persons Nonvoters ..	45.2	40.0	73.4	61.7	61.4	68.8
Rest of electorate	v 32.0	v 27.7	v 29.9	v 42.3	v 52.1	v 53.0

*Breakdown excludes 241 cases for which no basis for classification was available.

v: Greater than.

ʌ: Less than.

self-confidence made it likely that he would vote. But his weak concern for his self-interest in the outcome of the election made it difficult to appeal to him with detailed issue analyses. He could respond to the drama of a moral crusade and to the attraction of Eisenhower's personality.

Third, involved spectators and apathetic persons were particularly conspicuous among those who failed to vote. Apparently the low level of political self-confidence among these types could not be overcome either by the Democratic or the Republican campaign strategy in 1952.

It was postulated as a basic requirement for political consent that in a competitive election neither side should develop pervasive influence through the cumulative impact of the mass media and of interpersonal pressure. In summary, the data indicate that the campaign produced a competitive situation in which campaign pressure advantages of each side were counterbalanced by efforts of the opposition party. Whatever superiority existed in the canvass of the Democratic party, it was offset by the manifestly greater advantage of the Republicans in mobilizing their partisans by means of the mass media. As far as the mass media were concerned, radio, which had for years served the Democratic party as a counterweight to the Republican press advantage, was being effectively supplemented by television in 1952.

The sum total of these counterbalancing forces was of crucial advantage to the Republicans. To judge by inferences drawn from the analysis with which this chapter is concerned, the results from the mass media and the party canvasses were hardly so extensive as to constitute manipulation that might threaten the stability of the political system. However, a pattern of more effective and more extensive manipulation is suggested when the impact of the campaign is drawn broadly enough to include the concerted primary group pressures. Here lies a significant point in contemporary American political arrangements. The minority of the total electorate (21.2 per cent) which found itself under concerted primary group pressures was the main target for manipulation by the mass media. Yet a heterogeneous social order with high rates of geographical and social mobility does act as a limiting factor on concerted primary group pressures. Likewise, the lack of mass-membership political parties, often held to be a weakness of American institutions, adds to effective political competition in this context by limiting interpersonal pressure to more reasonable levels.

THE FINAL BALANCE: CONSENT VERSUS MANIPULATION

In this study of the 1952 election, an explicit theory of democracy formed the terms of reference for an analysis of data collected by the survey research method. A series of five criteria indicated the variables to be investigated. This chapter is an attempt to integrate our findings and evaluate how much consent was generated by the election. It is also an attempt to draw inferences about the policy problems of preserving and strengthening the election process in the United States, and thus to contribute toward making it less vulnerable to the threat of mass manipulation.

The same variables brought into focus in investigating the requirements for a democratic election can also serve to account for the pattern of the 1952 presidential vote. This was not our central objective. Yet the particular variables lend themselves to summarization by the "cross pressure" approach, now a traditional mode of analysis for political behavior data collected by the sample survey.

"CROSS PRESSURES" AND VOTING BEHAVIOR

Lazarsfeld, Berelson, and Gaudet first employed the "cross pressure" model in *The People's Choice*,[1] a study of 1940 presidential voting behavior in Erie County, Ohio. They sought to isolate a series of basic social group pressures on the individual which could be inferred from his social group memberships and affiliations. In particular, they were concerned with social class, religion, and residence as indices of political predisposition ("Index of Political Predisposition"). Upper social class, Protestantism, and rural residence, taken together, were group affiliations predictive of the Republican presidential vote; lower social class, Catholicism, and urban residence were predictive

[1] *Op. cit.*

of the Democratic presidential vote. The more the voter conformed to these ideal types, the more likely he was to vote in the predictive fashion. Individuals with mixed characteristics were conceived of as being under cross pressures. They tended to reveal a higher incidence of nonvoting and a greater degree of persistent political indecision. By contrast, those who were not under cross pressures were likely to resolve their political indecision in line with their group characteristics as the campaign progressed.

Campbell, Gurin, and Miller, in *The Voter Decides*[2] followed the same model of cross pressures in their analysis of presidential voting behavior in 1952. Instead of using social group variables they chose "attitudinal" variables. Party identification, issue partisanship, and candidate partisanship were the three used; these are essentially patterns of attitude orientation which were seen as pressures on the individual that motivated his voting behavior. The congruence of these variables is required for effective political behavior—either Democratic or Republican—and the effectiveness of their motivating force is reduced if there is conflict between them. As in the case of the Lazarsfeld, Berelson, and Gaudet model, cross pressure was seen as leading to nonvoting, political indecision, vacillation between parties, and the splitting of tickets.

Obviously these models are not being offered as the bases for constructing broad theories of voting behavior. They are empirical extrapolations of trends, and this mode of analysis can have high empirical relevance. But the cross pressure analysis requires some theoretical justification for stating in advance which and how many variables are needed. More important, the conversion of cross pressure indices into a more relevant theory requires some *a priori* assumptions as to the social and political conditions under which the importance of the independent variables in the cross pressure models will increase or decrease. The substitution of attitude variables by Campbell, Gurin, and Miller for the sociological variables employed by Lazarsfeld, Berelson, and Gaudet would still leave

[2]*Op. cit.*

this central problem unsolved, and without such assumptions it is hard to account for political change.

In a sense, the Lazarsfeld, Berelson, and Gaudet variables imply a more general theory. Social class, religion, and place of residence imply a social stratification overview of politics. The success of their index therefore depends on the relevance of social stratification considerations in any particular election. The fact that the Lazarsfeld index failed to work when applied to the national electorate in 1948 merely means that that was an election in which the assumptions of social stratification for national voting behavior could not be directly applied. (It could also have meant that the specific variables used for operationalizing this model were inappropriate for that election.) Despite the preoccupation of the 1952 election with international politics and the government corruption issue, there were strong overtones of politics along lines of social stratification. Thus, the "Index of Political Predisposition" had some predictive power when applied to the national sample of the 1952 electorate. For voters not under cross pressures to any marked degree, the index accounts for voting preference correctly in seven out of every ten cases:[3]

Index of Political Predisposition	1952 Voting Behavior			
	Score*	Eisenhower (Per Cent)	Stevenson (Per Cent)	Total Number
Strongly Republican...........	1,2	72.1	27.9	(290)
Moderately Republican	3	63.6	36.4	(236)
Moderately Democratic	4,5	55.0	45.0	(364)
Strongly Democratic...........	6,7	30.8	69.2	(133)

*The "Index of Political Predisposition" ranges from a score of 1 to a score of 7, and is based on the characteristics of urbanism, social economic position, and religion. The index is so designed that low scores should predict Republican voting and high scores should predict Democratic voting. See *The People's Choice*, *op. cit.*

Thus, it was necessary to reformulate the cross pressure approach in order to make it more theoretically relevant. It is

[3]The "Index of Political Predisposition" had somewhat more predictive power in 1952 than in 1948. See Morris Janowitz and Warren Miller, "The Index of Political Predisposition in the 1948 Election," *Journal of Politics*, 1952, pp. 710-27.

doubtful, of course, whether the cross pressure model could ever be completely satisfactory. It is based on the assumption that all the variables required for analysis can be observed by the survey research technique at the level of the electorate. Sociologically speaking, there is the entire process of political party organization by which candidates are selected and issues posed which defies research at this level. There are motivating factors of self-calculation which voters are unable to convey well to the survey researcher. Nevertheless, a series of major theoretical assumptions can be made for improving the cross pressure model.

The model ought to link together both social structure and social psychological variables. Social scientific research has underlined this assumption if the dangers of sheer eclecticism are to be avoided. Whereas *The Voter Decides*[4] postulated the independence of attitude structures from social structure, *The People's Choice*[5], and likewise this analysis, proceeded from the underlying social structure variables. The data at hand indicate, as could have been predicted, that for different social groupings the same social psychological predispositions had different political consequences. High political self-confidence meant a tendency toward Democratic voting behavior in the lower class, but a reverse tendency in the middle class. Thus, social psychological variables can be introduced into a social structure analysis of political behavior for refinement and fuller explanation.

When social psychological variables are used in the cross pressure approach, they need not and should not be thought of as pressures merely impinging on the individual voter. These variables can describe the proclivities and calculations of voters as active agents in the political arena. This is not to say that those proclivities are rational and conscious. Nevertheless, self-interest and self-confidence, as social psychological measures, help overcome the view that the voter is merely a passive element subject to external pressures.

[4]*Op. cit.*
[5]*Op. cit.*

The cross pressure approach should include variables that encompass the pressures coming directly from the political campaign. From the point of view of political scientists, party canvass and the political content of primary group pressures are essential in any composite cross pressure model. In most studies, the emphasis has rightly focused on variables that seemed likely to explain voting behavior in terms of underlying and persistent attitudes toward politics. But the data of this and other studies indicate the importance of immediate political pressures on a critical minority.

Thus, in putting our data into a more comprehensive model of cross pressures, it seemed fitting to use two types of variables; first, a measure of political predisposition, and, second, a measure of campaign pressure. With a simple combination of the specific measures of (a) political partisanship and (b) concerted primary group pressures, it was possible to account for the presidential vote with a high degree of accuracy, and to account simultaneously for the amount of nonvoting. The measure of partisanship, as defined, reflected underlying position in the social structure, as well as personal and family predispositions that become manifest under pressure of the campaign. Concerted primary group pressure was shown to reflect both formally organized and immediate personal considerations, as well as the appeal of the candidates.

In general, when political partisanship and primary group pressures coincided, it was possible to predict the vote in more than eight out of ten cases. More specifically, Republican partisans under concertedly Eisenhower primary group pressures produced a 95.4 per cent Eisenhower vote, whereas Democratic partisanship and pro-Stevenson primary group pressures produced an 80.1 per cent Stevenson vote (see Table XLII). Between the two extremes, these two variables established a symmetrical array of cross pressures. It is striking that the ratio of Eisenhower and Stevenson votes varied with the shifts in cross pressures as expected in each of the seven types.

At the same time, these variables of cross pressure related

TABLE XLII

POLITICAL PARTISANSHIP AND PRIMARY GROUP PRESSURES
IN THE 1952 ELECTIONS

Partisan Predisposition and Primary Group Pressures	Voting Behavior Patterns: 1948-1952			
	Pro-Republican Voting Behavior (Per Cent)	Pro-Democratic Voting Behavior (Per Cent)	Persistent Behavior Nonvoting (Per Cent)	Total Number
A. Republican partisans under concerted pro-Eisenhower primary group pressures	95.4	2.6	2.0	(153)
B. Non-Republican partisans under concerted pro-Eisenhower primary group pressures	83.6	9.6	6.8	(191)
C. Republican partisans under conflicting primary group pressures	68.8	11.0	20.2	(170)
D. Uncommitted electors under conflicting primary group pressures	36.2	27.1	36.7	(450)
E. Democratic partisans under conflicting primary group pressures	27.2	50.0	22.8	(430)
F. Non-Democratic partisans under concerted pro-Stevenson primary group pressures	12.8	72.3	14.9	(47)
G. Democratic partisans under concerted pro-Stevenson primary group pressures...	6.9	80.1	13.0	(115)

closely to nonvoting in a similarly symmetrical fashion, with nonvoting related directly to cross pressures.

Finally, individuals who were uncommitted in their partisanship and under conflicting primary pressures were, as expected, almost wholly unpredictable in their voting behavior. It was important for this cross pressure model that this group be divided into roughly equal proportions of Republican voters, Democratic voters, and nonvoters. Thus, this model, in contrast to the "Index of Political Predispositions," is applicable to the total electorate—voters and nonvoters—and not merely to those who voted. In an over-all evaluation of the election process, these findings on the influence of political partisanship and interpersonal pressures assume prime importance.

THE CONSEQUENCES OF POLITICAL COMPETITION

It was not, of course, the primary goal of this analysis to explain presidential voting patterns in terms of cross pressures. Our point of departure was a theoretical orientation of political science toward the democratic election process. Elections were seen as competitions by parties for popular consent to their leadership. The central concern was thus to learn how closely the 1952 election conformed to this ideal preconception. Any such preconception postulates a functional contribution which the election process must make to the political community if democratic institutions and practices are to be maintained.

As noted in the introductory chapter, political scientists have identified at least two alternative functional orientations toward the democratic process of elections. The "mandate" theories, which find their origin in the classical conceptions of democracy, postulate that the process of representation stems from a clear-cut set of directives which the electorate is able to impose on its representatives. An election is then a process of convenience and a way of ensuring that representatives will comply with directives from constituents. This preconception was rejected in advance as unrealistic because it assumed a level of articulate opinion on campaign issues not likely to be found in the United States. In fact, it is doubtful that such a level has existed in any democratic electorate since the extension of the franchise in the nineteenth century. The data of this study have supported the contention that mandate theories cannot be used as the basis for empirical analysis, regardless of their value as utopian goals toward which men may aspire. To the political philosopher, this finding must emphasize the equal futility of mandate theories as a *raison d'être* for basic beliefs or as a yardstick for policy recommendations.

The point of departure actually employed was the assumption that a democratic election is a process of selecting and rejecting candidates who are competing for public office.   The election campaign is thus a device for assessing leadership.   Five criteria were postulated for identifying the conditions under which competition would produce a decision based on consent rather than on manipulation.   These criteria were offered not as an exhaustive set, but as those most significant.   They made it possible to evaluate how much the conduct and outcome of the 1952 election added to the long-run maintenance of a democratic process of self-government.

It was our conclusion that the 1952 election campaign did result in political change in the presidential office, based fundamentally on a process of consent.   In applying each of the five criteria, the underlying process of consent could be clearly inferred.   In the absence of trend data for comparison with 1948, it was impossible to judge the relative increase or decrease in the balance of consent versus manipulation.

At the same time, these five criteria emphasized where and how much manipulation existed.   They pointed to a series of weaknesses in the election process; they revealed conditions under which such weaknesses would become aggravated.   These weaknesses are clearly profound enough to indicate that constructive measures are needed to discourage the type of competition that can only result in increased and dangerous manipulation.   It is very unlikely that these defects will correct themselves merely in the "course of events."   These criteria also pose the tasks of political reform that will be needed in the future to preserve and strengthen the democratic election process.   For purposes of summary and synthesis, we will discuss the criteria one by one.

1. *The quality of the election depends upon the degree to which competition produces a high level of citizen participation among all social groups.*

For the electorate as a whole, the level of voting participation in 1952 seems to have met this basic criterion reasonably well, if only because it reversed recent trends in voting turnout. The conclusion is well documented that the pervasiveness of competition penetrated deeply throughout the nation. In particular, the process of consent was enhanced by the South having its most competitive campaign in recent history.

Undoubtedly, the intensity of the competition added to the high level of participation; 61.6 million votes were cast, accounting for approximately 74.2 per cent of the potential "residential" electorate. This was far from the universal participation urged by some as a desirable goal. The criterion actually employed required more than a majority for consensus to exist, and for the essential stability of the political system; it hardly required universal participation. Universal participation might in fact have signified that the election process had become the only process for collective problem-solving, a most dangerous burden for the American election process to assume. Likewise, universal participation or even extremely high levels of participation would have implied that each party had no new resources to mobilize for solving new political crises. Nonvoters, if they are not overconcentrated in a particular social group, now operate as a cushion and an unknown which can inhibit extremists of both parties.

The data seem to indicate that the 1952 campaign was as intense and competitive as our democratic institutions could readily accommodate. Later conclusions under the second criterion dealing with social psychological predispositions lend further support to this observation. The fact that other democratic nations have and are achieving higher levels of participation is not directly relevant unless comparison can be made with the needs and potentials of American politics.

In an industrialized, stratified society, the level of participation by various social classes and minority groups is just as important as the over-all level of participation. But whereas the over-all level of participation was relatively satisfactory in 1952, voting participation in the lower-lower class and among Negroes was dangerously low. In the lower-lower class, nonvoting did not quite reach the halfway point (44.7 per cent), and, on a national basis, 67.3 per cent of the Negroes did not vote.

The implications of such a maldistribution of voting participation are clear. A consensus is incomplete and fragile which lacks the adequate involvement of one social class or ethnic group. A group that is persistently nonvoting carries the potential of a sudden entrance into the political arena which can severely strain the processes of political compromise. Such nonvoting weakens the ability of political leaders to offer and carry out legislation meeting group needs with confidence that their decisions are acceptable to all groups affected. Nonreliance on the electoral process by substantial social groups increases their availability to appeals of the demagogue.

Education is often cited as the key variable accounting for limited participation by the lower-lower class in political elections. Education is, of course, closely correlated with social class. However, formal education per se hardly constitutes an explanation for nonvoting, nor does it offer a specific approach for leading the lower-lower class directly to increased voting. The trend toward higher average education in the United States has not been accompanied by a rising level of voting. In certain respects, the reverse may even have occurred. Education is only an indirect index of the complex class tensions, social dissensus, and struggles for mobility in the United States. Many of those at the bottom of the social structure fail to make use of the election process as a device for bettering their chances in life, despite the wide possibilities that political action might hold for them. The explanation of the election behavior of the lower-lower class lies not only in political predispositions and attitudes that depreciate the significance of politics, but also in a pattern of social realities that render voting less meaningful to them.

By contrast, the upper-lower class displayed a much higher level of voting participation, very close though not equal to that of the middle class groups. This group does not represent the same danger to political stability that the lower-lower class does. Thus, there is a level in the social structure below which social position constitutes a danger to the political stability of the system. What variables, in conjunction, serve to identify that level? This point may be thought of as involving both income and status. There must also be variables to measure involvement with and understanding of the symbols and institutional processes of the community, such as belonging to voluntary associations, community activity, and self-respect.

In this view, proposals for strengthening democratic processes which demand redistribution of income along simple equalitarian lines must be rejected. Instead, the minimum problem appears to be that of setting income norms below which no individual or family group should be allowed to fall. Coincidentally, then, the income distribution best for a democratic political process resembles what some advocate as also desirable for full employment and a stable use of resources.

As far as status is concerned, recent trends in occupational structure have probably cut down further the absolute size of the lower-lower class. In the United States, the lower-lower class is already smaller than either the upper-lower or the lower-middle class. Yet for the utopian goal of a society without a lower-lower class—rather than a classless society—more change is required than the creation of higher minimum income standards. It probably requires a social structure in which income distribution and income expectations are linked more realistically than is now the case. Given the predispositions towards political processes found in this analysis, there is good reason to believe that such readjustments could be achieved by political action and governmental policy without creating destructive political tensions.

However, overcoming the disruptive political consequences of gross inequalities in prestige presents a problem which is infinitely more difficult and more baffling. The basic moral relations of the society are involved, especially as they relate to the status of Negroes. It is clear enough that the integration of Negroes in the social community involves basically different problems than the integration of other ethnic minorities. The data suggest that political action and governmental policies can influence this process greatly, but only through a more indirect approach than that for solving economic needs. Political action and governmental policies can only help bring about the conditions under which voluntary group action could result in changing the patterns of respect.

Both in redistributing income and in modifying moral and prestige values, crucial responsibility for maintaining and developing the democratic process rests with the conservative political elements. This is hardly unique in recent modern history. Their guardianship of the venerated symbols of authority and their powerful position in the American constitutional system imply that conservative agreement is needed and will set the rate of political change as long as democratic practices are followed.

2. *The quality of the election depends on the extent to which citizen participation is based on predispositions of high political self-confidence as well as on self-interest in the outcome of elections.*

The two dimensions of political self-confidence and self-interest in the outcome of elections were viewed as social psychological predispositions within whose limits competition would have effective consequences. The empirical findings indicate clearly that political self-confidence is a category distinct from the concept of self-interest in elections. Modern processes of democratic competition during election campaigns pose a constant danger that the average citizen will lack confidence to take part intelligently or be too confused to discern clearly where his self-interest lies, or both—and under such circumstances political decisions will degenerate for many into the mere conformity of a plebiscite.

The absolute levels of self-interest and self-confidence encountered were in part reflections of the specific measures employed. Only through a trend comparison of one election with the next can the full significance of such data emerge. Yet even for the 1952 election, comparisons between voting segments with different predispositions were revealing. Analysis in terms of self-interest and self-confidence indicated that the competitive process had penetrated to the periphery of the electorate. Those voting segments directly responsible for the political change in 1952, when compared with 1948 (D − R's, NV − R's, and D − NV's), had in each case a disproportionately large share of voters with weak self-interest and low self-confidence. This finding therefore raised serious concern about the effectiveness of the process of consent, especially since there is evidence from the data in this survey that deeper personality factors, in particular the authoritarian syndrome, are conditioning low self-confidence and the tendency to submit to political manipulations.

Interpretation of these findings depended on analysis of the class basis of the 1952 election. Eisenhower in effect destroyed the coalition of the upper-lower and lower-middle classes on which the New Deal was built. The Eisenhower vote was directly and progressively related to social class; the higher the social class, the greater the concentration of Republican votes. By contrast, the Democratic concentration rose as social class fell, with the exception of the lower-lower class, where the highest concentration of nonvoting for any social class reversed the trend line. Moreover, the magnitude of the gains for Eisenhower was also progressively related to social class, with the high social groupings registering the greatest shifts towards his candidacy. In the end, Eisenhower received plurality support only in the middle class, upper and lower, and among farmers, although Stevenson's margin of superiority in both lower class groups was small.

The consequences of the underlying social psychological predispositions were assumed to be, and were found to be, different for the different social class groupings. It was precisely those middle-class individuals whose democratically oriented predispositions were weak who constituted the bulk of the pro-Eisenhower changers. In the lower class, to the degree that social psychological predispositions were involved, there were indications that the shift to Eisenhower was based on high self-confidence. These findings show how important it is to specify social class when noting the relevance of psychological predispositions for explaining political behavior.

Again, the central issue for reform is not merely to increase political participation. Voting without properly based motivation holds inherent dangers to the political system. In recent years, there has been considerable agitation to increase the size of the turnout. It could be questioned whether these efforts, which rely heavily on the mass media and similar devices, represent a misuse of limited resources.

Concern with the size of the vote may well obscure the more important question of the function and the quality of the vote. The underlying belief, in a democracy, that everybody ought to vote, is indeed deep-seated, but it must be considered utopian. Reforms have been suggested that are designed to enhance the quality of the vote by modification of the social structure. Yet in terms of practical political reform, the important issue is to stimulate the participation of better candidates and to increase candidate competence. There are some indications that this point of view is growing and is supplying a more relevant rationale for educational and political groups.

In evaluating the level of voting turnout and its consequences, it is necessary to recall that Republican partisans tend to vote more regularly than Democratic partisans. This does not mean that the pressure toward extremist appeals and extremist tactics lies more with the Democrats, who seem to have a harder time mobilizing their partisans. The political complexion of the country, even after the Eisenhower victory, is still predominantly Democratic in partisanship. Therefore, again, the burden of responsibility for the conduct of the political process rests heavily with the conservative political elements, to the degree that the Republicans represent these conservative elements. Tht large size of the independent vote has acted as a partial inhibitor to domination of both parties by extremist factions; the danger of driving the independents into the opposition camp has ever been present. However, the question arises whether the size of the independent bloc has not grown too large for this function. Moreover, the weak ideological orientation of many in the independent group who wield the balance of power is another basic limiting condition, especially during periods of prolonged political tension. Self-restraint on the part of the party leadership is clearly required to retain the effectiveness of the competitive system.

3. *The quality of the election depends on the extent to which competition stimulates effective political deliberation on the issues and candidates and creates a meaningful basis on which citizens can make their voting decisions.*

In some particular opinion groups, the character of political deliberation over central campaign issues must be judged as falling short of the requirements for effective consent. This conclusion depends less on the analysis of attitudes toward specific issues and more on over-all orientations toward a sample of campaign issues. Specific issues were, of course, important for special groups.

Of the specific issues, governmental corruption, rather than internal communism, appears to have had the greater effect on voters for Eisenhower. Moreover, a range of important domestic issues revealed the extent of the division between Eisenhower and Stevenson voters. On the issue of social welfare activity by the government, consensus was high, as reflected by the fact that more than half of the Eisenhower supporters were willing to accept Democratic policies; almost 90 per cent of the Stevenson supporters endorsed the party stand. By contrast, ideological orientation with respect to labor presented a markedly different pattern in which a majority had no sort of crystallized pattern. Opinions on F.E.P.C. were highly differentiated, revealing only moderate differences between Republican and Democratic supporters.

Attitudes toward several aspects of U.S. foreign involvement divided Eisenhower voters from Stevenson voters almost as much as any single domestic issue. Korea emerged as a most critical aspect of the campaign deliberations. Despite Eisenhower's pronouncements, the original American intervention in Korea remained controversial. Moreover, Eisenhower represented a compromise position on current policy in Korea to citizens whose views differed markedly.

In order to judge the quality of citizen deliberation, an analysis of ideological orientations was made, employing four categories. There were "stalwarts" who supported the party position on almost all issues, "compromisers" who supported the party position on a majority of issues, "weak compromisers" whose support was limited to a minority of issues and who tended to have no partisan opinions on the remainder, and "ambivalent-neutrals" whose ideological outlook seemed to embody no partisan preference.

Each of these groups was assumed to have a distinct contribution to make to the process of consent. Traditional democratic theory has stressed the need for having sizable groups of party stalwarts for effective political competition. The absence of an articulated ideology among large numbers of the electorate has been viewed as a fundamental defect. The burden rests to some extent with the parties to pose issues that articulate with the personal ideological demands of such citizens.

Additional problems that have not received due emphasis in current democratic theory were also explored by this type of analysis. First, a balance between stalwarts and compromisers was felt to be necessary if both flexibility and consistency were to be realized. Both parties in 1952 secured some such balance. Second, the political climate of America today includes concern over the low level of deliberations among weak compromisers and ambivalents. This concern may be aggravated by rigidity among party stalwarts, if they grow in numbers.

It is, of course, disturbing that 29.5 per cent of those who voted were weak compromisers. Weak Republican compromisers voted two-to-one for Eisenhower, while weak Democratic compromisers gave a slight advantage to Stevenson. That such voting behavior was not completely random suggests that party-framed alternatives were at least partly effective. Yet, in order to appeal to these groups, both parties seem to have extended their positions by over-simplification and extremism.

Of even greater concern were the ambivalent-neutrals who constituted 16.5 per cent of the Eisenhower vote and 20.2 per cent of the Stevenson vote. For them, the campaign competition appears to have failed in linking together party-framed alternatives, personal ideological demands, and voting behavior. It is with special reference to these elements of the electorate that the growth of an ideologically rigid core of party stalwarts offers twin dangers. On the one hand, the party's programmatic goals may be fashioned in response to the ideological demands of stalwarts. On the other hand, the party's appeals to those with low levels of articulated ideology may accentuate sensational and demogogic themes. Thus, within each party, a gulf may arise between the followers-by-conviction and the followers-by-manipulation. From these considerations, it becomes imperative that the vitality of "party compromisers" be sustained if an ideological balance between flexibility and consistency is to be maintained.

These findings could also be summarized in terms of voting change. Those voters who were pro-Republican changers between 1948 and 1952 showed a markedly lower level of ideological orientation than did persistent Republican voters. A similar, but somewhat narrower, gap was present between pro-Democratic changers and persistent Democratic voters.

As opposed to the complex relations between campaign issues and the presidential vote, the link between candidate image and presidential vote reached an almost one-to-one correspondence. The expected link between imagery and presidential vote was not only high, but significant exceptions or even revealing deviations were missing. Does campaign competition, so closely linked to candidate personalities, offer a meaningful basis for political choice? This kind of campaign seems especially fitting when a president is elected for four years and no parliamentary form of government exists. However, the character of political consensus that rests heavily on candidate competition suggests inherent problems for representative government.

The remaining two criteria dealing with the mass media and interpersonal pressures are so closely interrelated as to warrant joint evaluation. A democratic election implies that both sides are able to make extensive use of the means of mass communications and to mobilize extensive interpersonal pressure by means of the party canvass and primary group relations. Nevertheless, the bulk of the electorate must be able to maintain an essential freedom of choice in registering political consent.

4. *The quality of the election depends on the extent to which limitations operate precluding either side from monopolizing or even exercising pervasive influence by means of the mass media.*

5. *The quality of the election depends on the extent to which the influence of interpersonal pressures operates substantially independent of the influence of the mass media.*

Analysis of the data on mass media exposure and involvement points to the general conclusion that in 1952 the fourth criterion for consent was fulfilled. Neither side was able to exercise such pervasive influence by means of the mass media. This does not mean there were no differential consequences for one party as opposed to the other, as a result of mass media impact on particular social groupings. On the other hand, the fifth criterion, involving interaction between the pressures of the mass media and daily associates, identified a process with important potentials for manipulation and some manipulative consequences.

In the mass media competition, Republicans had the initial advantage, since their partisans were more exposed and more involved. Likewise, the social class patterns of media exposure were to their advantage. However, television, which became a principal campaign medium for the first time, upset the simple formula, since it was able to reach the lower class groups so important to the Democrats.

With its greater political balance and accessibility and with its larger lower-class audience, television held the potential for countering the Republican-oriented press, with its larger middle-class audience. In this 1952 election, television, along with radio, began to perform the role traditionally assigned to radio alone by the Democratic party.

The mass media audience was also analyzed in terms of levels of political self-confidence and self-interest in elections, and in terms of political orientations. In many respects, these dimensions also indicated "built-in" limitations on the manipulative potential of the mass media.

Thus, when the patterns of exposure and involvement for the specific media were traced out, important inferences on impact could be drawn. But important as these consequences were for the Republican victory, the magnitudes involved again indicated an absence of pervasive influence. First, the mass media probably stimulated voting through the activation of nonvoters, and this increase seemed to be linked specifically to exposure to television and the press. Second, the mass media seemed to assist Republicans more than Democrats in mobilizing their partisans. Third, television played a special role by dramatizing a relatively unknown standard-bearer for the Democrats, and thus tended to prevent even more defection from the Democratic bloc than occurred.

The most important variable used in evaluating the fifth criterion on interpersonal pressure was that of concerted primary group pressures—from family and daily associates. It was in this respect that the power of the Eisenhower "personal crusade" was dramatically reflected. Desipte the preponderance of Democratic partisans in the population, 21.7 per cent of the electorate were under concertedly pro-Eisenhower pressure and only 10.7 per cent under concertedly pro-Stevenson pressure. "Concerted pressure" was defined to include uniform viewpoints among friends, co-workers, and family. Such concerted pressure showed a pattern of interactive effects conditioning the final vote. Pro-Stevenson pressure was linked to a 78.1 per cent Stevenson vote and pro-Eisenhower pressure was even more effective, 88.5 per cent of the time leading to Eisenhower votes.

As far as the party canvass was concerned, there was cumulative evidence that although the Democratic and Republican canvassers were roughly equal in extent and focus, the Democratic canvassers were somewhat more persuasive. This was a campaign pressure that offset but did not counterbalance the mass media advantage of the Republicans. Democratic canvassers were notably more successful in Democratic strongholds and among the uncommitted electorate. In addition, there were similar but less marked advantages in the canvass of the lower class, ethnic-religious minorities, low-confidence persons, and those with weak self-interest. The Republican canvass revealed almost no improvement in the ratio of Eisenhower to Stevenson voters among the canvassed portions. In fact, Republicans canvassing among the lower class, ethnic-religious minorities, Democratic partisans, and persons under pro-Stevenson pressures had to be judged as having aided the Stevenson cause.

But the full test of the fifth criterion required an examination of the interaction between mass media and concerted primary group pressures. The political relevance of primary group pressures, it will be recalled, was highlighted in the two-variable model of cross pressures—political partisanship and the primary group—which had considerable predictive power. The data indicated that concerted primary group pressure did not isolate the citizen from the impact of the mass media. In fact, it worked to reinforce the effects of the mass media rather than to counterbalance them. It is important to bear in mind the size of the electoral group which was under joint pressure from intense media involvement and concerted primary group politics. Of the total electorate, 21.2 per cent were in this set of circumstances. The overwhelming majority (90.2 per cent) of them voted, and their voting behavior conformed closely to the primary group pressures exerted on them. The danger lies in the possibility that the interaction of these two sets of pressures encouraged conformity to the preferences of daily associates rather than mature deliberation.

The manipulative potential of this combination of pressures is different from the one characterizing voters whose choices were based upon weak psychological predispositions or on incomplete ideological orientations. There the manipulative potential derived from a relative lack of free choice and an absence of pressures encouraging deliberation. The increase in concerted primary group pressures which could be generated through the development of mass political organization must be acknowledged, in the light of European examples. The current inefficiency in party canvassing efforts, which take a "shot-gun" approach, may not continue. But mass party organization translated into concerted primary group pressure could create real barriers to the development and maintenance of a genuine process of consent.

By contrast, for those under conflicting primary group pressures, the mass media transmitted the full range of competitive forces in the campaign. Neither party was outstandingly successful in its mass media appeals either to media fans or ordinary users when their daily associates disagreed politically. In the case of television fans not under concerted primary group pressures, there were interesting consequences. Of all the mass media involvement groups, only this group voted to Stevenson's advantage and this relationship cannot be attributed merely to the characteristics of the television audience.

In more general terms, when social psychological predispositions were investigated among those not under concerted pressure, Stevenson's appeals via the mass media were more persuasive than Republican strategy among effective citizens, whereas Eisenhower's appeals drew a disproportionate share of those who were highly self-confident but lacked a feeling of self-interest in the election outcome—the indifferent citizens. The Democrats were no more successful than Republicans in mobilizing involved spectators and apathetic persons. The absence of primary group pressure placed a sharp limit on manipulative pressures and opened the way for a more adequate competitive process.

Thus, the fifth criterion can be said to have been operative, although with marked limitation. The bulk of the population was not under concerted primary group pressures; and only where primary group pressures and exposure to the mass media converged could the danger to the process of consent be localized.

In summary, we investigated levels of participation among social groupings, social psychological predispositions, ideology, candidate imagery, and the various campaign pressures in order to assess the balance between manipulation and consent. In the view of the authors, the 1952 election was characterized by a process of genuine consent to a greater degree than their impressionistic estimates might have implied. Without the corrective of empirical data, political scientists face the inevitable problem of distinguishing between the typical and the readily observed. Campaign events could easily be cited which, had they become widespread developments, would have meant that the democratic process was in crisis. Through the sample survey approach, however, these events could be assessed empirically as to their impact and ramifications.

In using sample survey data, an analytical perspective had to be employed. Political competition gave us the frame of reference, and allowed us to incorporate important sociological and social psychological variables. Political apathy, as measured by participation and issue involvement, has been the basic concern of students using empirical methods to analyze electoral behavior. The results of this analysis may help to broaden that emphasis by calling attention to barriers to the process of consent of an opposite variety. These barriers derive from two of the sources highlighted by the investigation. First, there are the tendencies for ideological orientations to rigidify among portions of the party stalwarts. Second, there are the dangers stemming from the intense struggle that develops around the candidates and their public imagery.

Ideological rigidity and over-intensified candidate competition present serious implications. In the political struggles, the parties must make wide use of the mass media and interpersonal political pressures. There is the danger that political parties will intensify their tactics to influence these voters who have proven especially susceptible to manipulative campaign practices because of low political self-confidence and weak self-interest. But equally important is the need for political parties to accommodate themselves to the predispositions of those with rigid ideologies and those who are predominantly candidate-oriented. Over-intensification of the political competition is certain to create a gulf between the various portions of the electorate and thereby weaken the viability of any political decision that emerges. Over-intensification of the political competition is also certain to have a disintegrative effect on the compromise-oriented groups, with their "built-in" predispositions against manipulation. Fundamentally, the election could be judged as a process of consent only because of specific compensating and self-limiting factors. In planning for and assessing future elections, it would be a grave error to deny that manipulative pressures were present.

TECHNICAL APPENDIX

In September and October of 1952, and in the six weeks after the election, the field staff of the Survey Research Center of the University of Michigan interviewed a nation-wide cross section of adult citizens living in private residences. Employing regional stratification, controlled selection, and an area probability sample design, the survey achieved approximately 90 per cent response. The full technical details of the sampling procedure are contained in the basic report, *The Voter Decides*,[1] by Angus Campbell, Gerald Gurin, and Warren E. Miller.

The data of this study represent the national "residential electorate," with a sample of 1,614 persons having been interviewed both before and after election day. The "residential electorate" could have been 83 million adults; approximately 15 million persons of voting age were by definition excluded—including all noncitizens, institutionalized persons, military personnel, and persons lacking a permanent private residential address. Through failure to meet voting requirements of one kind or another, the bulk of this marginal population probably did not vote in 1952. Moreover, since the total vote was 61.6 million, about 21.4 million nonvoters were included in the "residential electorate."

SECTION 2: OPERATIONAL DEFINITION OF PARTISANSHIP

In developing a measure of partisanship, two considerations were given special attention. First, partisanship was defined as a long-term commitment in favor of the symbols of a major party. Thus, it had to be defined operationally to reflect persistent and generalized orientation rather than the transitory and particularized views people developed toward the major parties as the campaign progressed. Second, it had to be defined operationally to reflect more than a casual preference for

[1] *Op. cit.*

identifying oneself as a Republican or Democrat. To restrict partisanship to a perspective reflecting long-term commitment, this measure included the three dimensions of (*a*) family party preference, (*b*) party of own first vote, (*c*) current party identification. Partisanship was thus defined as consistency among all three elements.

A few persons named one party as that of their parents but claimed current and initial voting allegiance to the opposite party for themselves. This was the only mixed pattern of responses for which an exception was made. It appeared justified, since in recent works on the dynamics of personal allegiance to cultural symbols, the view has been gaining support that allegiance through an easy process of generalization and incorparation of parental values is less strong and persistent than allegiance to symbols based upon revolt from family authorities.[2]

SECTION 3: OPERATIONAL DEFINITION OF GEOGRAPHICAL STRONGHOLDS

The national sample used in this study was drawn from sixty-eight primary sampling units, each consisting of one or two counties. Official election statistics were collected for these various units and the pattern of party success was identified for each unit from 1936 through 1948.

Nearly one-fifth of the national sample lived in "Republican strongholds"—meaning that, in presidential elections from 1936 through 1948, Republicans had either carried these localities consistently or the trend toward Republican dominance had reached a point by 1948 where at least 55 per cent of the vote was then recorded in the Republican column. At the opposite extreme were another two-fifths of the population—half of them Southerners, half non-Southerners—living in "Democratic strongholds." Except for the Dixiecrat vote in 1948, these localities had been at least 53 per cent Democratic in every presidential election from 1936 through 1948. And

[2]See Herbert Goldhamer, "Personality and Public Opinion," *American Journal of Sociology*, January, 1950, pp. 346-54.

finally, about two-fifths of the sample came from localities where the two parties were evenly matched. In the last four contests for the presidency, each party had demonstrated in these "competitive" areas that it could garner between 46 and 54 per cent of the two-party vote.

SECTION 4: OPERATIONAL DEFINITIONS OF MASS MEDIA EXPOSURE AND INVOLVEMENT

Two measures of mass media impact were employed in this study—one of media exposure and one of media involvement. The measure of exposure established the number of media which a given person regularly used "to follow the campaign closely." The measure of involvement distinguished the television, radio, and press "fans" from ordinary users and non-users.

The "media fan" was defined as a person who not only used a particular medium "to follow the campaign closely," but also designated that medium as his "most important source of political information." The "ordinary user" was defined as one who acknowledged the importance of a particular medium as his source of campaign news but who did not use that medium regularly to follow campaign developments closely. Non-users neither used a medium to follow the campaign closely nor acknowledged the importance of mass media as sources of political news. By combining the media involvement measures, it was possible to make a summary comparison of media fans, ordinary users, and nonusers without distinguishing between television, radio, and newspaper segments.

SECTION 5: OPERATIONAL DEFINITION OF SELF-INTEREST IN ELECTIONS

Convictions of self-interest in elections must, it was felt, embody not only the view that one's personal interests would be maximized through the victory of one side over another, but also that the democratic election process per se, regardless of who won, was important to one as a citizen.

Operationally, these considerations led to the requirement that, to qualify as exhibiting strong self-interest, a respondent's convictions about the importance of elections must have been *at least* as strong as his convictions about the importance of which side won. Further, we had to face explicitly the theoretical question of what terms of reference should represent the basis for calculations of "self-interest"; we had to break away from the false distinction between "selfish" and "altruistic," which is so often implied by the reference to "self-interest." We deliberately allowed a respondent to qualify as manifesting strong self-interest in two quite different ways, as far as the second criterion was concerned—that he must see a basis for maximization of his self-interest in the victory of one side rather than the other. Thus, whether the citizen conceived of his self-interest diffusely (in terms of nation-wide consequences) or specifically (in terms of his family's financial well-being) or in both ways, he was considered to have met this criterion. Strong self-interest by no means implies the opposite of altruism. It is more properly contrasted with weak self-interest, in the sense that the respondent fails to manifest adequate awareness of the importance of the election as a *means* to his personal ends. For such a person, the inference could not be made that he was involved in the democratic process in a rational and calculated way.

To score as having "strong" self-interest in elections, one must have responded to at least one of the following two questions by expressing the opinion that "important" differences would result:

(*a*) "Do you think it will make a good deal of difference to the country whether the Democrats or the Republicans win the election this November, or that it won't make much difference which side wins?"

(*b*) "Do you think it will make any difference in how you and your family get along financially whether the Democrats or Republicans will win?"

In addition, to score as having "strong" self-interest, one must have agreed with *both* of the following statements:

(*c*) "The way people vote is the main thing that decides how things are run in this country."

(*d*) "Voting is thé only way that people like me can have any say about how the government runs things."

The rationale for scoring (*c*) and (*d*) requires elaboration. Many citizens, thinking of their personal experience, would agree that voting was (*c*) the main way and (*d*) the only way for them to assert political influence effectively. In fact, the vast majority of those who agreed with (*c*) also agreed with (*d*). Such people met the full test; their self-interest in elections was both strong and focused.

Other citizens, although agreeing that voting was (*c*) the main way of being politically influential, might judiciously have denied that voting was (*d*) the only effective way. However strong the general political self-interest of such citizens might have been, their response to (*d*) indicated that they recognized other effective means than voting for asserting their self-interest. Lacking the required focus on democratic elections as the appropriate means, these persons did not meet the full test. To qualify as having "strong self-interest in elections," the respondent had to agree with both (*c*) and (*d*).

SECTION 6: OPERATIONAL DEFINITION OF POLITICAL SELF-CONFIDENCE

Feelings of political self-confidence, it was thought, must embody more than the view that the election processes of a democracy make it possible to influence the course of public policy. In addition, the individual must have shown that he was capable of discerning the issues and alternatives presented by the election, and finally the conviction that his personal participation made a difference.

Operationally, any rejection of three out of the four statements below was sufficient to satisfy all of these requirements. Accordingly, the line between high and low self-confidence was drawn so that all persons scoring "high" disagreed with at least three of the statements used. They were:

(*a*) "Sometimes politics and government seem so complicated that a person like me can't really understand what's going on."

(*b*) "People like me don't have any say about what the government does."

(*c*) "I don't think public officials care much what people like me think."

(*d*) "So many other people vote in the national elections that it doesn't matter much to me whether I vote or not."

SECTION 7: OPERATIONAL DEFINITION OF SOCIAL CLASS AND ETHNIC-RELIGIOUS GROUPINGS

Constructing a class index is a complex task and a mechanical breakdown by occupation of the voter was not considered adequate. Social class is closely linked to occupation, but it is more than occupation. In addition, a significant number of the electorate have no occupation; that is, they are either housewives, retired, unemployed, or students.

Therefore, the respondent was seen as a member of a household, and wherever feasible and appropriate, assigned a position in the social structure on the basis of his own occupation or that of the head of the household. For the retired and the unemployed, additional rules made possible the assignment of a position in the social structure.

On the basis of occupational groupings, the lower class consisted of the following occupations: skilled, semiskilled, unskilled and unemployed. The middle class consisted of the following occupations: professional, managerial, clerical, and protective service. Within each class, further division was made on the basis of income so that the total population could be divided into four groupings; lower-lower, upper-lower, lower-middle, and upper-middle.

In developing a measure of ethnic-religious groupings, Negroes, Jews, and Catholics were first distinguished. Taken together, these represented the so-called "minorities." Among the remaining majority of Protestants, a distinction was made between "nominal Protestants" and "church-going Protestants."

SECTION 8: IDEOLOGICAL ORIENTATION TOWARD CAMPAIGN ISSUES

The individual questions were:

(*a*) *Governmental Social Welfare Activity:* "Some people think the national government should do more in trying to deal with such problems as unemployment, education, housing, and so on. Others think that the government is already doing too much. On the whole, would you say that what the government has done has been about right, too much, or not enough?"

(*b*) *FEPC:* "There is a lot of talk these days about discrimination, that is, people having trouble getting jobs because of their race. Do you think that the government ought to take an interest in whether Negroes have trouble getting jobs or should it stay out of this problem? Do you think we need laws to deal with this problem or are there other ways that will handle it better? Do you think the national government should handle this or do you think it should be left for each state to handle it in its own way? Do you think the state governments should do something about this problem or should they stay out of it (also)? "

(*c*) *Taft-Hartley Labor Law Revision:* "Have you heard anything about the Taft-Hartley Law? (If yes) How do you feel about it— do you think it's all right as it is, do you think it should be changed in any way, or don't you have any feelings about it? (If should be changed) Do you think the law should be changed just a little, changed quite a bit, or do you think it should be completely repealed?"

(*d*) *U.S. Foreign Involvement:* "Some people think that since the end of the last world war this country has gone too far in concerning itself with problems in other parts of the world. How do you feel about this?"

(*e*) *U.S. China Policy:* "Some people feel that it was our government's fault that China went communistic—others say there was nothing that we could do to stop it. How do you feel about this?"

(*f*) *U. S. Entry into Korean War:* "Do you think we did the right thing in getting into the fighting in Korea two years ago or should we have stayed out?"

(*g*) *U.S. Korean Policy Before the 1952 Election:* "Which of the following things do you think it would be best for us to do *now* in Korea?

(1) Pull out of Korea entirely? (2) Keep on trying to get a peaceful settlement? (3) Take a stronger hand and bomb Manchuria and China?"

The classification of response patterns used in measuring the extent of "party-framed" ideology was as follows. "D" indicated agreement with the Democratic administration's policy, "R" indicated disagreement with the Democratic administration, and "X" indicated acceptance of neither party's position, or no opinion:

Republican stalwarts	RRRRR
	RRRRX
	RRRRD
Republican compromisers	RRRXX
	RRRXD
	RRRDD
Weak Republican compromisers	RRXXX
	RRXXD
	RXXXX
Ambivalent—neutrals	RRXDD
	RXXXD
	XXXXX
Weak Democratic compromisers	DXXXX
	DDXXR
	DDXXX
Democratic compromisers	DDDRR
	DDDXR
	DDDXX
Democratic stalwarts	DDDDR
	DDDDX
	DDDDD

SECTION 9: OPERATIONAL DEFINITION OF CANDIDATE IMAGERY

The content analysis of candidate imagery allowed us to characterize the respondent's attitude toward each of the candidates and what they stood for politically. These characterizations were either favorable (pro), unfavorable (con), or neutral (none). The candidate imagery patterns are shown below:

			Image of:	
			Eisenhower	Stevenson
Strong pro-Eisenhower	(1)		Pro	None
	(2)		Pro	Con
Mild pro-Eisenhower	(3)		Pro and con	None
	(4)		Pro and con	Con
	(5)		Pro	Pro and con
Ambivalent	(6)		Pro	Pro
	(7)		Pro and con	Pro and con
	(8)		Con	Con
No candidate image	(9)		Con	None
	(10)		None	None
	(11)		None	Con
Mild pro-Stevenson	(12)		Pro and con	Pro
	(13)		Con	Pro and con
	(14)		None	Pro and con
Strong pro-Stevenson	(15)		Con	Pro
	(16)		None	Pro

SECTION 10: OPERATIONAL DEFINITION OF INTERPERSONAL PRESSURE

In developing a measure of "concerted primary group pressure," the following questions were employed:

1. Could you tell me how your friends voted in the elections? Did they vote mostly Republican, mostly Democratic, or were they pretty evenly split?

2. How about the people where you work? Did they vote mostly Republican, mostly Democratic, or were they pretty evenly split?

3. (If married) How about your (husband) (wife)? Did (he) (she) vote Democratic or Republican?

4. (If not married) How about your family? Did they vote Democratic or Republican?

Those classified as under "concerted pressure" in one political direction were identified by their explicit responses to all of these queries. Those not under concerted pressure included, therefore, all respondents who did not meet the requirement of consistency in reporting the politics of friends, co-workers, and family as being alike.

INDEX